THE Love CLINIC

THE *Love* CLINIC

How to Heal Relationships in a
Christian Spirit

THE REVEREND DR. SHERON C. PATTERSON

A Perigee Book

A Perigee Book
Published by The Berkley Publishing Group
A division of Penguin Putnam Inc.
375 Hudson Street
New York, New York 10014

Copyright © 2002 by Sheron C. Patterson
Book design by Tiffany Kukec
Cover design and art by Charles Björklund

Black Pearl edition: February 1999
First Perigee edition: October 2002

Visit our website at www.penguinputnam.com

Library of Congress Cataloging-in-Publication Data

Patterson, Sheron C., 1959–
    The Love Clinic : how to heal relationships in a Christian spirit / Sheron C.
Patterson.—1st Perigee ed.
        p. cm.
    Includes bibliographical references.
    ISBN 0-399-52815-6
    1. Interpersonal relations—Religious aspects—Christianity.   2. Love—Religious
aspects—Christianity.   I. Title.

BV4597.52 .P38 2002
248.4—dc21
                                                                    2002029288
Printed in the United States of America

10 9 8 7 6 5 4 3 2 1

DEDICATION

This book is dedicated to my loving, supportive husband, Robert L. Patterson Sr., who through our years of marriage manages to show me each day that love never fails.

TABLE OF CONTENTS

Foreword   ix

Acknowledgments   xi

ADMISSIONS OFFICE   xiii

Chapter 1:
MISTAKES THAT SINGLES MAKE   1

Chapter 2:
THERE IS HELP FOR THE HOOCHIE   12

Chapter 3:
WHEN DOGS CONFESS, THEY
TURN FROM PREYING TO PRAYING   22

Chapter 4:
WHEN IT'S OVER, IT'S OVER   32

Chapter 5:
HOW LONG MUST I WAIT?   39

Chapter 6:
YOU'RE NEVER TOO OLD FOR LOVE   46

Chapter 7:
TO SHACK OR NOT TO SHACK?   53

Chapter 8:
BEFORE YOU SAY "I DO"   64

Chapter 9:
I DON'T LOVE YOU ANYMORE   75

Chapter 10:
SAY WHAT?   84

Chapter 11:
CAUGHT IN THE ACT   94

Chapter 12:
YOU CAUGHT YOUR SPOUSE IN THE ACT   104

Chapter 13:
YOUR MARRIAGE FAILED, NOT GOD   113

Chapter 14:
KEEP IT HOT   121

Chapter 15:
I STILL DO   130

Chapter 16:
SINGLE PARENT BLUES   139

Chapter 17:
SAINT BY DAY, FREAK BY NIGHT   147

Chapter 18:
MY BABY'S DADDY   158

Chapter 19:
THE INVISIBLE LIFE CAN BE SEEN,
IF WE OPEN OUR EYES   167

Chapter 20:
YOU CAN RUN, BUT YOU CAN'T HIDE FROM AIDS   176

Chapter 21:
WHEN LOVING YOU HURTS ME   183

Chapter 22:
WHY DOES IT HURT SO BAD?   190

Chapter 23:
RING AROUND THE CLERGY COLLAR
RINSES CLEAN WITH CONFESSION   200

Chapter 24:
JESUS IS THE ONLY HIGH YOU NEED   211

PROGNOSIS   218

Endnotes   221
Index   231
About the Author   237

FOREWORD

As advice columnist for *Essence* magazine for the past 15 years, and having received thousands of letters concerning relationships, I know the Love Clinic is on time.

Dr. Patterson invited me to conduct a Love Clinic in Dallas. I came away from that event certain in the knowledge that I had been a part of a true love revival. The spiritual depth of the session took place when a young woman said she had twenty-six items listed that she expected from a potential mate. A spiritually insightful brother responded, "But, Sister, there are only ten Commandments."

The Love Clinic is a reality-based concept. Dr. Patterson's essays reflect the basic truth. There is a message for everyone in each literary composition.

As senior pastor of the St. Paul United Methodist Church, Dr. Patterson is a visionary and a true woman of God on a mission of salvation. I predict that the Love Clinic will become a national touring event that will change the hearts and minds of men and women across the nation and restore family values. The Love Clinic is spiritually correct: Love is the answer no matter what the question is. Political correctness hasn't gotten us anywhere.

We are standing in this new millennium looking for an answer to the age-old question: Am I my brother's and sister's keeper? Dr. Patterson's response is: Yes. And I agree. I am a sister psychologist who says "yes" to the spirit within.

Not only is Dr. Patterson saying yes, she has written a book that will keep us in divine order while we try to re-order our lives with love principals to heal our relationships. Pastor Patterson possesses Mosaic leadership, and has allowed the words of her mouth and the meditation of her heart to all come together in this book that is filled with essays for our deliverance. If testimony is indeed good for the soul, this book is that spiritual feast we've been waiting for. Amen.

Gwendolyn Goldsby Grant, psychologist, advice columnist for *Essence* magazine, TV talk show expert, inspirational speaker, and author of *The Best Kind of Loving*.

ACKNOWLEDGMENTS

The Love Clinic is a combined community effort that came together with support from many people. I owe my greatest appreciation to the Lord Jesus Christ. I praise God for my supportive congregation, St. Paul United Methodist Church in Dallas, Texas.

I'd also like to express my gratitude to:

- The Love Clinic Community Board members for their loyal and enthusiastic support, and many, many hours of long work.

- State Farm Insurance Company for their corporate underwriting support of the Love Clinic on Tour, and the Love Clinic Youth Summer Camp.

- Radio stations and radio personalities for spreading the news of the Love Clinic over the air, and for serving as guest moderators. A special thanks goes to Dallas station KRNB 105.7 radio and the nationally syndicated REJOICE radio. I am forever indebted to Willis Johnson of KKDA radio for endorsing the Love Clinic idea and helping me to launch this cutting-edge, community-based ministry.

- The print media for including us in articles and news briefs. A special thanks goes to Mollie and James Belt, owners of the *Dallas Examiner*, for their support. This book includes many excerpts from my columns that they print on a regular basis.

- Community churches for supporting the vision by sending members and hosting us.

- Christian mental health professionals for taking their valuable time to assist me in counseling.

I am indebted to Sylvia Dunnavant for initiating the Love Clinic in book form, I am extremely grateful to my literary agent Janet Manus for believing in this project, and I appreciate the exemplary editing work of Sheila Curry Oakes, my editor at Penguin Putnam Inc.

ADMISSIONS OFFICE

Welcome to the Love Clinic Admissions Office. We examine patients with broken, bitter, bruised, and torn relationships. The situation usually requires immediate attention, complete with blood work and X-rays. We also offer preventative work. Some relationships are healthy and strong. They benefit from a pat on the back and encouragement.

We always have Good News. This is not just any clinic. This is the Love Clinic where the restorative power of Jesus Christ reigns. In this place, the pharmacy is full of faith, hope, forgiveness, grace, and mercy. The Bible tells us that healing and full recovery are possible in the name of Jesus. As you enter the Love Clinic you should come expecting a blessing.

The doctor is in. Under the auspices of the ultimate healer, Jesus Christ, I specialize in restoring, reviving, refining, and redefining many types of relationships. The primary relationship is between you and God, followed by you and yourself. All other relationships—husband and wife, boyfriend and girlfriend, parent and child—hinge on our relationship to God.

Since 1983, I have devoted much of my life to the specialized ministry of Christian relationships. It began with singles ministries in the 1980s, and grew to include premarital and marital ministries in the 1990s. During that time I wrote two books and countless articles on the topic. I witnessed Christian men and women struggling with relationships as I traveled the nation teaching and preaching about God's plans. They were active in their churches, yet they struggled to experience what God has for them. I soon deduced that churches were not teaching the basics of love. This is not an indictment of all churches or pastors, but simply the reality that some pastors are unwilling or unable to preach and teach on controversial issues such as fornication, adultery, and teen pregnancy.

The Love Clinic is the physical manifestation of a vision that God poured into my spirit in 1995 as I studied for a doctoral degree in biblical male/female relationships at Perkins School of Theology at Southern Methodist University. God spoke as I read intricate and complex theses and research data in the seminary library. God's message? Take this knowledge to the streets, empower the masses to help themselves, teach the saints of God what real love is, and steer them clear of Hollywood's tainted versions. Thus, the Love Clinic was born out of the understanding that I must teach God's people to love.

The Love Clinic began accepting patients in November 1995 in the sanctuary of a Dallas, Texas, church where I was senior pastor. I did not use sugar-coated rhetoric. We've learned that the contemporary, sometimes raw reality is the most efficient equipment available. Church people are experiencing the same problems as the rest of the population. They need fast, effective help. They need the truth given straight—no chaser. I write bluntly and boldly. If you are easily offended, take an aspirin before you proceed.

The live Love Clinic is a two-hour seminar in which we focus on the most current issues affecting dating, marriage, and parenting relationships. People from all denominations, races, and age groups come because they are hungry for biblical guidance on contemporary issues. They are seeking a fresh Word from God about healing relationships.

Each session opens with prayer and praise time. I present the biblical foundation for the particular issue. Love Clinic has three ground rules.

1. Everybody's got something wrong with them.

2. Don't laugh at other's problems—they could be yours tomorrow.

3. There are no dumb questions.

Then we plunge in. For the next two hours God's powerful presence is felt. Then a preselected panel testifies on how God has moved in their life on this topic. The Holy Ghost comes by and the tongues of the congregation are loosened and confessions stream forth. The healing comes in the form of diagnosis and prescriptions that are offered to those in need. Altar call, prayer, and anointing conclude the session. It is a powerful time indeed!

I have an urgency about my practice. As a pastor and a relationship expert, I want us to move forward without being trapped by false definitions of love. I offer a prophetic Word of

Hope in each essay as to how we and our churches can find love. We all deserve better love. The time is now.

Within this book you will find 47 cases of church folk and the church's situations. Some will make you laugh, some will make you cry, some will make you shake your head and suck your teeth. These are composite characters of people helped in public Love Clinics and in my private counseling practice. The names have been changed.

Each case contains a diagnosis, prescriptions, and prayer, because we believe in the life-altering power of prayer. The Scriptures cited throughout the book are from the updated New American Standard Bible (NASB).

Imagine that you are sitting in the church sanctuary, filled with God's people, each with a different issue. The adulterers tend to gather on the left, fornicators are sprinkled through the middle, to the right are folks in abusive relationships, and the front row is full of parents in peril. Lean forward to hear and watch the saints come to the microphone to tell their stories. You will have a myriad of emotions as the dramas unfold. Remember, God is able.

THE
Love
CLINIC

Chapter 1

MISTAKES THAT SINGLES MAKE

If you are like most singles, when it comes to mistakes in the love department either you've just made one, you've just gotten out of one, or one is headed your way. Relationships can be a minefield and mistakes will occur, but they can be corrected. On the one hand, loneliness, fear, desperation, jealousy, and insecurity loom and lurk in every person you meet. On the other hand, the potential for love, fulfillment, joy, and peace reside there too.

One false move and singles may find themselves wounded by love. The Love Clinic wanted to offer singles an easy-to-read road map to a difficult to attain destination—successful relationships. Here are ten of the most common mistakes that singles make.

1. Carrying emotional baggage from one relationship into the next. These singles don't take the time to heal between relationships.

2. Lacking personal boundaries. This is seen in people who have no self-knowledge, self-control, or self-esteem.

3. Being overly influenced by family and friends. These singles are unable to cut the apron strings and act independently.

4. Possessing a high desperation level. These singles lack principles, and will date indiscriminately.

5. Being constantly attracted to the wrong type of person. These singles sabotage any hope for happiness by seeking out intentional mismatches.

6. Expecting your date to be perfect, while lacking perfection yourself. Such people are not able to be satisfied with anyone.

7. Preferring to date married people. Singles who date someone else's spouse keep themselves in a state of upheaval both in heaven and on earth.

8. Relying on sexual intercourse to get or to keep a person interested. Singles who use sex as their strongest offering get burned eventually.

9. Selecting someone outside your faith. A person who is not on the same page with you religiously is trouble from the start.

10. Refusing to learn lessons from former relationships. Foolish singles hate their history, rather than studying it.

Many of us wouldn't recognize love if it grabbed us by the lapels and hugged us. This is because we've been hurt by love and have a distorted sense of reality. As a result of all the hurting people out there, being a single adult looking for love can be a treacherous journey. The church has been the historical meeting ground for singles. The holy grounds of church are still a valid and safe gathering site, especially if one's heart is in the right place. Yes, the religious arena has been abused by wolves and wolf-ettes in sheep's clothing, but God's house is still the best place to meet or at least look.

∞ Case 1 ∞

Lena came to the microphone with tears in her eyes. She said, "I am a 40-year-old woman, and for the past 20 years I have prayed the same prayer to God every night. I have asked God to send me a husband and God has ignored me. Why is God doing this to me? All of my other friends are married with children by now—and look at me. I've done all the right things, but still no man."

Bubbly and heavyset, Lena was a sister on top of the world careerwise. She was a physician who was widely admired by her colleagues, and had the financial security of Fort Knox. She came from a long line of doctors. Her father was the first doctor to integrate the city's hospitals, and her uncle had done the same in another city. Her brother had gained national recognition for a recent organ transplant, and her cousin had just finished medical school with honors. Lena was born and bound to succeed. Her inability to secure a husband was the only blank space on her stellar record of achievement.

"It makes no sense that I can restore health to men, but I cannot find a man for marriage. What is the mistake that I am making?" she asked. "I meet men all the time at the hospital or at civic gatherings. They seem interested, yet after a few dates, they disappear and never call back. I am starting to get a complex."

Due to her economic status Lena didn't just date men, she bought men. She picked them up in her red Ferrari and also picked up the tab for the evening with her Platinum Visa card. She was in a pathetic cycle of meeting men, showering them with her largesse, and losing them.

∽ Diagnosis ∽

"Lena," I said, "you are having your own personal pity party—and it's time for God to crash it. Your blessings have become your burdens. I celebrate your personal and career accomplishments. When I need a physician I'd love to have a sister like you to work on me. But your blessings are out of control, and have turned you into a professional sugar momma. The word is out on the streets that you will give men anything they want, any time that they want it. They are using you.

"You are mothering and smothering them with your money. Being a mother/smother type is a good way to chase off the men with promise and attract the weak, wicked ones. Acting like your partner's momma gives him a loud message: You want him to feel happy because of what you are giving, you want him to be satisfied because of what you are providing, you want him to feel comfortable because of what you are doing. In other words, you want to be his whole world. The attitude that you are conveying as a woman is 'I'm everything to you. How can anyone else be anything?' "[1]

Lena, along with other women, seems to be feeling pressure to marry. We've heard the grim statistic that only some 25 percent of single sisters will marry.[2] We hear about the male/female ratio imbalance. And as a result we hear a voice that says grab up the first available man we see.

∽ Prescription ∾

Calm down and relax. When we make frantic frazzled moves, we make mistakes that could have been easily avoided. To relax and calm down, is to trust God to the utmost. If you are not careful, the desire for a man will supercede your relationship with Jesus. If you do not monitor and contain your interest in marriage, God will become a stranger to you. To avoid this, you need to learn to separate your faith from fairy tales.

We all were raised on fairy tales, or little stories of promise and goodness. One of the most popular pieces of fiction for a girl admonishes her to keep her room clean, behave properly, make good grades in school, never sass her elders, and in return, a handsome man on a beautiful horse will someday appear, sweep her off her feet and marry her. They'll ride off together into the sunset, and their life will be perfect. This is a fairy tale for many, many women. If we pin all of our hopes on this conclusion and it fails to materialize, we feel like failures.

Somehow our faith got tangled up in the fairy tale, and God has become the majestic distributor of men. If we do all the right things, a man will appear. This is not how faith works. Our faith gives us the ability to persevere whether we have a man or not. Our faith informs us that, with the Lord, we will have a great life because there is a greater God inside of us. So my sister, hold on to your faith.

Additional sage advice for singles comes from one on the front line. Dr. Suzan Johnson-Cook is a nationally known preacher who married later in life and faced some of the same issues faced by many singles. Her advice concerning men is this: First of all, learn how to celebrate men. Whether they work with you, provide routine services, or sit across the aisle from you at church, focus on reinforcing them in small ways. Discover that special glint in a man's eye when a woman pays him a compliment for a job well done.

Second, notice when men you come in contact with grow and improve. Provide them—fathers, brothers, uncles, cousins, friends, employees, and colleagues—with opportunities to improve themselves. Make sure that the men in your life now are growing as you are growing.

Third, don't hide your success, but enable the men in your life to handle it and be proud of you. Let them know how, even in small ways, they are part of your success.[3]

∞ Case 2 ∞

Cedric, who was a small man, came to the microphone to talk about a big mistake he was dealing with. "I am in the midst of something that initially seemed like a tiny issue to me. Now the issue is an out of control monster. I am dating a gorgeous young lady. We are compatible, we are made for each other. The problem is, she is not a Christian. In fact she does not believe in God at all," he said looking at me incredulously.

"Her beauty overwhelmed me at first. When I first found out that she was an agnostic, I thought, how can a woman who looks this good not know the Lord Jesus Christ? God obviously broke the mold with her. Our relationship is right in all the other areas. She was a friend first. We did not rush. We've invested lots of time with this bond. She has all the qualities that I wanted in a wife. She just does not know Jesus. But she said that she might change after we marry but she is not certain," he said.

Cedric is 35, and divorced. His first marriage was to a young woman he grew up with in youth ministry at church. That two-year marriage ended with drama and fireworks when he caught her cheating with the youth pastor. He understandably has wounds that have not healed yet. "I know that men are not supposed to show hurt or feel pain, but that divorce almost took me out," Cedric admitted. "I started doing stuff, bad stuff, that I'd never done before, like drinking. Before I knew what was happening I'd have a couple of six-packs of beer in the car with me after work. I needed the beer to help me make it through the night alone."

Cedric's behavior is not rare. In a study of divorced men, a portion of them initially used drugs or alcohol to cope with the pain of divorce. Men deal with feelings of loss by engaging in self-destructive behavior. Paradoxically, although the substance abuse relieved the men's emotional pain, at the same time it resulted in adverse consequences.[4]

Cedric is a counselor at an abused children's facility. He has deep compassion for hurting and suffering people. He met his current girlfriend through his work. She was an abused child and now she volunteers at the children's facility. The two of them share interests and are very similar in temperament and personality. To outsiders they appear to be an ideal couple. He is struggling with the reality that his love may be a mistake.

"I know what the scriptures say about dating those who do not know Jesus. My parents have spoken on it, and spoken on it. But they don't know how I feel. I followed all of the rules when I got married the first time. My ex-wife was reared in the church, just like me, and she still cheated on me—with a pastor! I see no need to put too much stock on a person's faith level. Their heart is all I need to know about," he stressed.

Both of Cedric's parents are pastors, and they instilled in him the necessity of marrying a Christian. Cedric's struggle is all the more real because his faith is a major part of his past, present, and future. He has a suppressed but intense interest in ordained ministry. His current relationship places him at odds with what he has known all his life.

☞ Diagnosis ☜

Cedric's connection to his girlfriend seems like love, but it sounds like missionary dating to me. "Missionary dating" is when Christians date non-Christians, and they hope to convert them. Be aware that you are playing with fire. A non-believer might show an interest in God in order to date you. If the relationship fails, that person's faith is likely to falter. And what if you think you've fallen in love? Where will your loyalty be then? To be in love is not necessarily to be in the will of God.[5]

Cedric may be in a rescuer mode as well. This is equally as dangerous, because he may be expecting to save or rescue his girlfriend either from her painful past or from her godless state. As he seeks to salvage her situation, he may lose his own. Remember the words from Matthew 5:13: *You are the salt of the earth; but if the salt has become tasteless, how will it be made salty again? It is no longer good for anything, except to be thrown out and trampled underfoot by men.*

Persons who choose to live without God do not have the capacity to love you the way that you want and need to be loved as a follower of Christ. I am not saying that they are inferior or evil. I know this is a harsh statement, but only those who know Christ as their savior are capable of loving you with the love of Christ. There is no other way around it.

∽ **Prescription** ∾

Pain from the divorce seems to steer Cedric a little off-base. God gives us the spirit of discernment to show us who is good for us, and who is not. You can know the Word, but is the Word in you? Are you hearing what God is saying? Here is a helpful chart comparing God's voice to Satan's voice. It's important to learn the difference.

"GOD'S VOICE	SATAN'S VOICE
Stills you	Rushes you
Leads you	Pushes you
Reassures you	Frightens you
Enlightens you	Confuses you
Encourages you	Discourages you
Comforts you	Worries you
Calms you	Obsesses you
Convicts you	Condemns you"[6]

I offer four basic steps to Christian dating.

1. Look for a friend, not a meal ticket, a sex partner, or a stepping stone for climbing the social or corporate ladder. *A friend loves at all times* (Proverbs 17:17). I saw a bumper sticker that read, "If you're rich, then I'm single." Beyond the humor in this saying lies the terrible possibility

of dating and perhaps marrying someone who has lots of
cash, but who makes you sick.

2. Date persons with similar Christian convictions. This way
you will not have to defend your faith, or compromise
your beliefs to impress or to keep a date interested in you.
*Do not be bound together with unbelievers; for what part-
nership has righteousness and lawlessness, or what fellowship has light with darkness?* (2 Corinthians 6:14).

3. Keep God first in the relationship. One of the great mys-
teries of all human relationships is that relationships themselves can become stronger when they are not made an
end in themselves. This has a special relevance to the relationships between male and female. Attend church together. Pray as a couple. Study the Bible together. All of
these activities can be a means of strengthening the indi-
vidual as well as the relationship in the Word of God.
*Commit your works to the Lord and your plans will be
established* (Proverbs 16:3).

4. Maintain high moral standards. Celibacy is a real possibility for single persons. Celibacy is abstention from sexual
intercourse. When celibacy is incorporated into dating relationships, each person is afforded the luxury of getting
to know the other on many important levels, such as personality, temperament, and character. Developing a heavy
physical attachment in the early stages of a relationship
can cloud and confuse the other basic concerns. *Therefore
I urge you, brethren, by the mercies of God, to present
your bodies a living and holy sacrifice, acceptable to God*
(Romans 12:1).[7]

We ended this session by thanking God for success in the midst of relational failures. I told the group that with God we can be supported through these challenging times. The key is learning how to lean on God. In Jude 1:24 we read, *Now to Him who is able to keep you from stumbling, and to make you stand in the presence of His glory blameless and with great joy, to the only God our savior through Jesus Christ our Lord, be glory, majesty, dominion and authority, before all time and now and forever.*

Let us pray

Dear God,

We singles will stumble and fall in our quest to find love. As we go about this task keep us in the hollow of Your hand and safe from dangers seen and unseen. As You keep us close to You, bring us to the person that You have selected as our mate. We trust You and You alone.

Amen

Chapter 2

THERE IS HELP FOR THE HOOCHIE

She saunters into worship service on Sunday morning with one thing on her mind—and it ain't Jesus. She is there to see and be seen. And once she has captured the attention of the men, she schemes for their money. Their cash will cover her rent, car payments, shopping sprees, and beauty bills. She is a hoochie—a woman up to no good in God's house.

A hoochie is a woman who uses her body to collect material gain from men. She will do whatever it takes to entice them to buy for her. In turn she cares nothing about them, and sets her sights on the next wallet. A hoochie can be 18 or 80 years old. She can be clad in an inexpensive spandex dress, or she can style in a $2,000 Chanel suit.

Terrible? Shameful? Get over your disdain—they are everywhere. Think about your church for a moment. Mentally review the women you saw in the congregation last Sunday. Didn't you see the sister dressed for the nightclub instead of Sunday worship? Don't you remember the woman who hounded the visiting men by smothering them in the fellowship hall? How does the church respond? Most of the time, eyes buck, heads wag, and teeth are sucked. Other times, lusty grins and double takes affirm a hoochie's skeezer ways. Occasionally an older, seasoned sister, full of Holy Ghost boldness, will pull the hoochie into a quiet hallway and say, "Baby you can't come in here with a skirt that short and sit in the front row. You need to change your ways!" I praise God for their boldness, but these women are rare. Usually hoochies are allowed to pursue their destructive ways because we are confused about appropriate expressions of materialism, faith, and relationships.

Hoochies are not a contemporary creation; they've been around for ages. Biblically speaking, Hosea 4:14 in the Old Testament refers to cult prostitutes, women who engaged in ritual sexual acts in idol-worshipping temples. These prostitutes worshipped pagan gods such as Baal and strived only for personal pleasures. The resemblance to our modern-day sisters is real. They may not engage in sexual acts in the church, but they certainly have covered the preliminaries.

Where do hoochies come from? What happens in a hoochie's life that causes her to sink to this depth? A hoochie's perverted, distorted understanding of who she is allows her to see herself and her world through the lenses of consumerism and self-preservation, often at the expense of others. She uses her body to gain goods from men. The type of man who is drawn to her also has a perverted, distorted sense of self. These men, along with the hoochies, have misunderstood God's purpose for them. As a result, a pattern of sluttish behavior is rewarded and repeated in our churches. There is culpability on both sides. The

Good News is that they don't have to stay that way. There is help for the hoochie. And that help is Jesus!

∽ Case 1 ∾

One sister, we'll call her Lisa, admitted that she is wrestling with memories of her former life as a hoochie. This 19-year-old college coed is known by many at her church because she sings in the choir and participates in the young adult ministry. She blends in with the church crowd because of her sweet and innocent girl-next-door look. Her black hair is cut so it waves and curls for days. Her light skin tone is most desirable, by those who favor the high-yellow look. In other words, she keeps the fellas in a frenzy. Most of her life men have given her things to make her happy and keep her interested. She habitually cared little for them. Her looks brought in the loot. She was not seeking a relationship, but access to credit cards and possessions.

"All my life I've looked and leaned on a man, you know? I believed that if a man is a man he shows it by buying. He puts things on my back," she said. "Growing up, the music taught me how it should be. I had to have the 'Bling Bling' [eye-catching jewelry]. And I had to be the 'Queen B.' Rappers like Lil' Kim and Foxy Brown were my role models. They know how to work a man over to get exactly what they want, when they want it. It's an acquired skill, and I was good at it," she boasted.

"My mom and dad don't know about my hooching. They think I am the sweetest daughter in the world. They think I bought all that stuff I was wearing at the mall. What they don't know won't hurt me. Church men were the easiest to roll on. They were sweet and unsuspecting. I dressed to catch the eyes of church men," she said. "My skirts had killer splits that made men melt. My specialty was the low-cut blouse and push-up bra on Communion Sunday. I lingered at the altar rail for a special laying on of hands when the pastor came by. My body was my calling card," she recalled.

"Praise God! I have been saved from that lifestyle," Lisa continued. "I got tired of the using, the lying, and the running around all the time. I felt cheap when I used the men. God had a better plan for me and I was certainly on Satan's road. It was nobody but the devil in me. If you knew the places I used to go and the things I used to do just to get an Emanuel Ungaro suit, or a Prada bag. Yeah, I got the high-priced goods, but they got the best of me. I did not win, the devil won. My spirit and my soul were filthy rags," she confessed.

"The problem is that I really miss the life. I felt like a queen with all the attention. My self-esteem was high, I knew that I was cute! But I knew what I was doing was wrong. Sometimes I wish I still had men offering me the fancy dinners and nice clothes. How do I stay strong in the faith, even though I enjoy the benefits of my past?"

∞ Diagnosis ∞

Lisa needed to understand that newness in Christ means releasing the old self, no matter how much *fun* it was. We all want nice things. Lisa needed a strategy for getting those nice things for herself.

I told her, "Lisa, by all means we want you to remain strong in the faith. We want you to remain on the Lord's side. The problem is that, as soon as we are sold out for Jesus, all hell breaks out in our lives. Satan does not want you to live completely for Jesus and so he creates a dissatisfaction in your spirit. He creates a feeling of not having enough, and not being enough so that you will step out of your God-commitment and turn back to his ways. And the truth is that you are more than enough with God. We find our completeness in God. God is the teammate we need on our team."

The Lord is my light and my salvation; Whom shall I fear? The Lord is the defense of my life; Whom shall I dread? (Psalm 27:1). With a clear and unwavering commitment to Christ, you can stand strong in the face of temptation and resist the desire to go back to the old life. And why go back anyway? What is the real benefit of being taken care of by a man? That's the lifestyle of lazy women. It's a form of slavery. I've seen so many women stuck in the materialism trap. They think that as long as their man is buying them gifts, they have it made. This is far from the truth.

∽ Prescription ∽

"Lisa," I said, "There is nothing wrong with wanting and having nice things. We all enjoy being pampered. The key for you is to give yourself permission to first take care of yourself rather than looking for a man to do it all. I believe that seeking the gifts was your attempt to experience power. You were seeking self-worth through men, who primarily wanted you as a sex object. It was a losing game. We women have personal power. When we give it to men in exchange for gifts, we lose it and become powerless in their eyes and our eyes."

Why do we women give up our power? We don't believe that we need it, but we do. Sisters, our power is our ability to get things done for ourselves and for others on our timetable.

Personal power is built on our belief in ourselves, personal determination, and the ability to set and achieve goals. Too many women don't use their power; they give it to the men in their lives. Why? Some have never seen a woman use her power. Others think that the only power we possess is between our legs. For Lisa, her personal power can turn her life around—if it is based on Jesus.

∞ **Case 2** ∞

Nicole, a 42-year-old real estate broker, had a suave penchant for relieving brothers of their cash. In her camel-colored, tailored suit with eyes and swing-bob hairstyle to match, Nicole is legendary around her church for the men she runs like clockwork. Beneath her cool exterior, Nicole is a complex sister on the verge of a breakthrough. She is almost ready to let this lifestyle go.

"Yes, I work hard every day, but my money stays in my pocket," she said. "It is the man's job to handle all of my needs. If he is a real man, he will be able to pay for my car, my condo, and all my bills. Without money, he will be without me. There is no need to change, I have a system that works," Nicole said matter-of-factly. "I don't see the role of Jesus in this section of my life. It is completely separate. What is the big deal?"

I responded, "The big deal is that using men is not what God wants from us. Men and women were not created to use each other. We were created to co-exist in harmony. Draining a brother of his money is not godly. At some point the Lord will tap you on the shoulder and say 'wait a minute, this is not right.' God talks to us all the time. We simply tune out the message, and let the devil have complete control. Has God tapped you on the shoulder yet?"

Nicole admitted, "Well, yes. Maybe that was God talking to me through the last guy, Bill. I used him up and threw him away, but this time it got to me. Bill thought that I loved him. I guess he had a reason to. I told him that I loved him, but he should have known that I was lying. Hell, we weren't in a relationship. We were just dating. He wanted to get all serious and stuff. Started wanting to go to church together. He was about to ruin all my action at church. He was supposed to be a man on the side, on the down low. But no, Mister I Love You, said 'let's get married, here's a big diamond, here's a full-length mink coat, here's a trip to Paris.' He thought I loved him. I told him, 'Well guess what?' He was wrong. I loved his money. When I ended that fake-love shopping spree, I had accumulated all I wanted. Mainly, I just wanted away from him. I remember the night that I ended the relationship. His eyes didn't look right. It looked like a vacuum cleaner hose had sucked the life out him. Too bad, so sad. I changed my phone number, ignored him coming to my door, changed the locks, and moved on to the next man."

But all of a sudden, Nicole paused. "The guilt fell on me like a 100-pound weight. I said, 'Lord, why do I feel responsible about this? I've used men before, and tossed them away like an empty soda can, and didn't look back. Why am I feeling pain this time?' Memories flood my mind. Memories of the times my daddy would promise to come and take me shopping, or to the movies, or just for an ice-cream cone. And I'd get all excited about time with my daddy. Momma saw me all hyped and every time she'd get real quiet and start to cry. He and my mom never married, but he said he loved me. I wanted to love him, but I never had the chance. Daddy left me hanging. He left his little girl sitting on the steps outside waiting for him till it was dark."

Tears were flooding Nicole's face. She had loosed her truth and that was a turning point in her life. The truth has a way of setting us free because it shows us what's really been going on. We choose to dwell on what we'd like to have going on. As I always say, "We've got to face it before we can fix it." Nicole did just that. Now we were making progress. "I'm hurting," she said. "The past hurts. Can the Lord do anything for me?"

⨳ Diagnosis ⨳

"Yes," I said, "God can fix whatever is wrong in our lives. God can make it all right." *Peace I leave with you; My peace I give to you; not as the world gives do I give to you. Do not let your heart be troubled, nor let it be fearful* (John 14:27). "The anger inside you is eating you alive—if you don't first purge that from your system there won't be anything left for God."

Anger serves as a barrier between us and others. It may seem safe to keep others at bay, but living on lockdown is a terrible way to live. We stew in poison, marinate in hatred, and anger saturates our souls.

Nicole's way out is to forgive her father. Once she forgives her father, she can forgive all the other men she encounters, too. The anger she has for her dad spills over into her relationships with men. She is forcing them to make up for what her dad did or did not do. Please understand what forgiveness is. It is not allowing what her dad did to be OK. What her dad did to her was wrong—there is no excuse for his actions. Forgiveness is not letting him off the hook. Rather, forgiveness lets her off the hook so that she can emotionally move on with her life. *Not returning evil for evil or insult for insult, but giving a blessing instead; for you were called for the very purpose that you might inherit a blessing* (1 Peter 3:9).

As Nicole returned to her seat, she responded, "I'll try. If the Lord can turn me around, I'll go."

∽ Prescription ∽

Churches are unwitting hoochie factories. They have produced and created the hoochie mentality for generations because of the second-class role that women have been forced to play.

> Institutional religions, echoing the patriarchal world in which they have thrived, have not only placed women beneath men on the hierarchy of being and value but also have failed to convince wombed and breasted women that they image the life-giving Deity in profoundly symbolic ways.[1]

Yes, church is the place where women go to feel good about themselves, but it also lowers our self-esteem because churches are based on a male-dominated or patriarchal mind-set. In these environments, women have difficulty developing and maintaining their positive self-value because their sources of personal power and validation are constrained by sexism. Women frequently hear "let the men lead, women can't serve on this committee," and "only men can be pastors here." As a result, they seek power where they can find it.

Hoochies such as Lisa and Nicole exist within the church because they have been socialized to behave this way. Pastoral care professor Carrol Saussy has written on this topic:

Within patriarchal society, women have been educated to believe that a woman's central task in life is winning a male partner— "the prize" who will be protector, provider, and father of her children . . . Only when a woman has come to believe in herself and in other women is she truly ready to share life with an equal partner . . . Reframing singleness is one of the many chores of confronting patriarchy . . . [2]

Let us celebrate God's strength and power to remake us for the better. In Psalm 51:10–13, we read, *Create in me a clean heart, O God, and renew a steadfast spirit within me. Do not cast me away from Your presence and do not take Your Holy Spirit from me. Restore to me the joy of Your salvation and sustain me with a willing spirit. Then I will teach transgressors Your ways, and sinners will be converted to You.*

Let us pray
    Dear God,
    Open our eyes to the value we have in You. Relieve us of fleshly living. Help us to walk by faith and not by sight. Stop the maddening dance of money that we find so delightful. Let us walk as whole men and women with You.
    Amen

Chapter 3

WHEN DOGS CONFESS, THEY TURN FROM PREYING TO PRAYING

He is all dressed up and ready for church. His suit is Italian. His shirt is Egyptian cotton. His shoes are alligator, dyed to an exotic hue. And his mind is brimming with slick schemes and tricks to trap the women eagerly waiting in the pews. He is a dog—a man who deceives women. And he is in God's house looking for his next bone—a naïve churchwoman. We are not male bashing—some churchgoing men behave more like snakes than saints. They are more ruthless than righteous. They may have a cross around their necks, but they are not carrying Christ in their hearts. They may shout "Amen" one second, but they may whisper an invitation to the backseat of their car in the next breath.

How do you spot a dog in the pews? Does he lead women on? Does he say one thing and do another? Does he date multiple women, in or out of the same church, at the same time?

Does he have the gift of talking celibate sisters out of their chaste convictions, then dumping them once he has scored? Does he have babies at churches all over town?

There is a long tradition of churchmen behaving badly. Like their hoochie counterparts, dogs also have biblical roots. In 2 Timothy 3:6 we learn about the forerunners of dogs: *For among them are those who enter into households and captivate weak women, weighed down with sins, led on by various impulses.* There are weak, silly women in churches, and this does nothing but exacerbate the situation. Some male attitudes suggest if women are stupid enough to give these dogs sex, money, and other delights, why not partake of it? Some men rationalize that they can't help themselves: "It's the dog in me." Some men keep score and applaud such conquests, as notches in their belts. Church becomes their hunting ground because church chicks are easy to get over on.

Doggish men abound in churches for at least three reasons. First, a reporting system for scamps does not yet exist. A churchwoman would be too embarrassed to admit that Brother So-and-so had fleeced her. She cannot possibly go tell the pastor or the deacon that the man she fornicated with last night refuses to even acknowledge her today as they sit side by side in the choir. Who is there to inform in the church hierarchy that the Scripture-quoting man she thought she could trust with her credit card did not purchase the tie that they'd agreed on, but bought an entire suit, and a designer one at that? There is no one to tell.

Second, many Christian men are dogs because they are victims of their society and culture. They do not know what it means to love a woman. Street lure exhorts that only weak men show concern and compassion, fidelity and trust. Societal institutions have not conveyed to men that women are significant, and that sane relationships with them are critical. When this misogyny is combined with sexism (religion's long-term companion) and biblical phrases are used to keep women relegated to the second-class, churches become cruel minefields waiting for unsuspecting sisters to stumble into them.

Thirdly, men do not receive enough encouragement or support for treating women with respect and dignity. There is an unwritten code among some brothers that says "dog or be dogged." If a man does not outmaneuver the woman in the relationship, he will be called a *punk*—one who let his feelings get in the way.

> Success with women is important to many men because they are engaged in covert competition with other men. They believe that through success they will avoid ridicule and will be considered "hip." In the process the women become the target and the game becomes an end in itself rather than a means to an end.[1]

It is no accident that *dog* when transformed and turned around becomes God. That's what happens to men when they understand who God truly is. When dogs confess, they turn from preying to praying.

⮐ Case 1 ⮑

Tre, a 32-year-old computer programmer, is a tall, handsome man who would make a woman look twice. Every Sunday he is in church, and from the outside looking in, he was a man after the heart of the Lord. Little did we know, he was after something else. Tre was a man who honed the skill of emotional distance down to a fine art. He knew how to be involved with a woman, but not involved with her. His body was there, his words were there. But his heart was a million miles away.

"Churchwomen are easy marks for dogs. We know how to handle them," he stated boldly. "There I was, well dressed, handsome, and standing with a Bible in my hand. Those sisters were so blind that they could not see that I was the proverbial wolf in sheep's clothing. I was a dog with no shame in my game. Everyone was doing the same thing. I'd meet my boys in the church parking lot and we'd plot and scheme," he explained. "I was involved with four women at the same church, and none of them had a clue that I was cheating. I would meet one woman at the 8:00 a.m. service, the second in Sunday School, the third at the 11:00 a.m. service, and the fourth at Wednesday night Bible study. Some of the older men knew what I was doing and they helped me pull the whole thing off smoothly."

Tre grew up an only child in an emotionally cold home. His mother showed him little or no affection. She was too busy working three jobs, and his father was a long-distance trucker who was only home a few days a month. He had to chart his own pathway in the confusing world of relationships. Tre is a smooth talker. He talks to women, and they believe that they are the only woman on the earth and that God has sent him just for her. The silver-tongued gift among men "makes it easier for them to create an initial impression of genuine feelings, and thus they readily enter relationships with women."[2]

One day all of Tre's smooth talking backfired. The women he was dogging ganged up on him. Their feelings had been demolished, and they felt abused and used. They exploded on Tre on the church grounds. "They jumped me," he said, embarrassed. His arm was broken in the melee, and he sustained head injuries that required stitches.

While he was in the hospital recuperating Tre reflected on his actions. "I was hurting women, I had gotten myself hurt, and most of all, I was hurting my relationship with God. I broke down and cried as I thought about all that I was doing. There was no good reason for any of it. I was tired of playing like a boy in elementary school. But I knew that only God could provide the strength I needed to carry myself like a man," Tre recounted.

∞ Diagnosis ∞

The Lord moves in mysterious ways. What looked like Tre's ending was really his beginning. Have those wounds healed yet? He knows that he was wrong for running games in God's house. His doggish ways were prolific and time-consuming. I praise God that Tre was open to the movement of God in his life and he allowed God to come in and turn things around. Here's the truth. Tre is an expert at emotional distancing. His emotions were foreign to him and he had no idea of what to do with them. He has a fear of getting too close to any woman. He wasn't taught how to open up. He was exploring his manhood the best way that he knew how—keeping women at a distance. I'll bet he was encouraged to start as many relationships with as many women as he could at the same time. His smooth talk brought the women to him, but his doggish ways provoked them to violence.

From a proportion standpoint it works like this. The more women a guy is dealing with, the least likely they are to get close to him. According to author William July, "As a general rule, the more a man is getting around, the lonelier that man really is on the inside. It's easier to hit and run. Stay in the streets and never have any feelings."[3]

Tre is not alone. Men have lots of reasons for avoiding intimacy. Some say it scares the hell out of them.[4] Others use the excuse of their careers. They claim that they have to focus on maintaining their spot on the fast track of employment. Another one is the "I've been hurt and don't want to be hurt again line." They carry around old wounds and parade them like prizes. Girls grow up talking about their feelings, but boys grow up playing sports and are not taught to build relationships.

∞ Prescription ∞

"Experiencing emotional intimacy means dealing with your inner man," I told Tre. "You will need to confront who you are inside. In order for you to do this, I recommend a love hiatus. That means no women for at least six to eight weeks. You need to spend time examining yourself and handling those tender, hidden feelings that you've buried inside. Ask yourself these questions: Who am I? What brings me joy? What makes me sad? Your emotions are not your enemy. God gave them to you for a reason, so that you could express yourself."

If your family of origin did not give you what you needed in the area of emotional support, that's no excuse for today. None of us can go around whining about what mama or daddy did or did not do. We are responsible for our own today and tomorrow. The fear of dealing with feelings or becoming vulnerable may be based on the saying that "people take your kindness for weakness." But the Apostle Paul writes about this in 2 Corinthians 12:10 *for when I am weak, then I am strong.* Real love makes you strong.

∽ Case 2 ∾

The lives of some men assume a canine characteristic for an assortment of reasons. The doggish ways can be fueled by many factors. Intimacy issues are one. Another can be misogyny— hatred of women. Jonathan did not want to say anything, and looked angrily at the microphone and me. But something compelled him to speak. Sometimes we know that something is wrong, so we reach out. Jonathan was reaching out, finally. He had hit the bottom. This Brooks Brothers suited-down and wing-tipped man looked like the epitome of the Wall Street crowd. He spoke with a crisp diction and sharp articulation. "Do I look like a dog? Do I talk like a dog? I think not," he answered himself. "Yet this very morning, my wife took our children and left me because she said, I had dogged her long enough. How could I be a dog? I put a roof over her nappy head. I gave her a car to drive. When I met her she was riding the bus. I've got her shopping at Neiman Marcus when all she knew was Wal-Mart. My career has the two of us in an income-bracket so high it gives her a nosebleed. How am I a dog?"

Jonathan had an arrogance about him that flashed like a neon light. He behaved as if the world owed him something. Maybe it did. His momma told him so. From the time he was small, Momma made sure that the world knew her son was number one. Jonathan wanted for nothing during his childhood. Any request that fell from his lips sent his mother scurrying to the mall. So frequent were his demands and so easily were they met by his mother that he developed a hatred for her. She was weak. She was too compliant. In return his mother increased the gifts to try to win her son's love. He loved her, but he loathed her too.

"My wife never really appreciated me," Jonathan ranted. "All she had to do was keep the house clean, provide the meals, and take care of the children. Is that so hard? She could not do anything right. The house was filthy. The food was unacceptable, and our children are in a deplorable condition. She is an unfit mother and an unfit wife."

⤳ Diagnosis ⤳

Jonathan sounds as if he may be a misogynist—a man who hates women:

> The misogynist may be consciously drawn toward women and "likes" them—until a woman becomes his intimate partner. Then something switches. While the misogynist still feels "love" toward the woman, his behavior is discrepant. One minute he is bringing roses, the next he is throwing food on the floor . . . [5]

Jonathan's wife called him a dog because of the way he treated her, not for what he had purchased for the home or the income bracket they were in. He described his wife with a lot of animosity and contempt in his voice. His home may be a pressure cooker. The wives and children of misogynist "feel as if they are walking on eggshells all the time, never knowing when the switch will happen again."[6] To keep the family in chaos, misogynists use their strength from their perceived position, authority, physical stature, or symbols or achievements to compensate for their lack of character. "They use force and overpower their families to get things done. This only reinforces his inner weakness, since it allows him to rely on external rather than internal strength."[7]

I told him, "If you cannot see the damage inflicted on your family by your abusive behavior, you are in denial." Jonathan's wife did him a favor when she took the kids and left. She brought him out of denial. It was the only way to get his attention and to shake up his self-centered world. The separation is what it will take to break through his denial of what's really going on in his world.

∞ Prescription ∞

For Jonathan the only way out of his misogyny is to change his entire way of thinking. He will have to understand his world and all those in it differently. This means giving up the notion that he is the victim. He is not. He is the perpetrator. He may think that "he has given and given and is to be commended for putting up with such a burdensome wife."[8] This arrogant viewpoint will keep him reacting and waiting for others to change. To change himself, he must become a "responsible chooser—someone who is not merely reacting to things around him, but is choosing his behaviors."[9]

Most of all he will need a therapist or counselor to guide him through this very long process of change. Only a counselor can help him with areas such as

- Learning how to take orders rather than to give them.

- Learning how to express anger appropriately without bullying or manipulating.

• Learning how to ask for help when under stress.[10]

We closed this session by joyfully acknowledging the power of God to assist us when we are tempted. Matthew 26:41 tells us, *Keep watching and praying that you may not enter into temptation; the spirit is willing, but the flesh is weak.*

Let us pray
  Dear God,
  Have Your way in our hearts today. Whatever You discover that should not be there, please take it away. Attune our ears to Your plan for manhood. Direct our feet in the ways that please You. Mold our lives that they might edify You. We want to be worthy vessels.
  Amen

Chapter 4

When It's Over, It's Over

What a wake-up call! You finally figure out that the one you love does not love you. The signs were there: She never returns your calls. He forgets your birthday when you remembered his and purchased a gift. He dodges you after worship service. She makes dates and never shows up. He calls you by another woman's name. You found cuff links in her car, and you don't even own cuffs. She has that distant look in her eyes. It is over.

Do you have the strength to end the relationship? Can you pick up the two-way and send a message that says "I'm dropping you like a bad habit"? Or "things aren't working out"? Or "let's just be friends"? Or do you trudge along praying, fasting, and begging God to change that person's heart? It's time to stop being a fool for love. We believers have a track record for accepting the worst and forgiving, forgiving, and forgiving until we lose sight of our own self-worth. The Lord wants us to forgive and forget, not look stupid.

Sometimes we love the wrong one and wind up being played. If this describes you, don't get mad, just get out of the relationship. Singles need a keen and astute spirit in the dating world. Matthew 10:16,. . . *be as shrewd as serpents and innocent as doves,* is appropriate. The dove keeps them mellow and the serpent won't let them be taken. In the singles world as in the marriage world, some of us prefer a known hell to an unknown heaven. I've counseled men and women determined to let the joker they were dating destroy them. Desperation does strange things to people.

∞ Case 1 ∞

The problem for Trina, a 21-year-old manicurist, is that her man is MIA—missing in action. "I can't find him. I page him, I call him but there is no response. Half the time he does not answer his pager or his cell. He is out of communication," she said. Trina comes from a family that places importance on a woman having a man in her life at all times. Trina's mother always had a man in her life. Even though it was a different man every month, at least she had a man. Trina's three sisters operate in the same way.

"My boyfriend never spends time with me," she complained. "He is always with his boys. He only comes to spend time with me late at night. Then it's too late to go out and have any fun. I'll wind up cooking and then we'll watch television. It's always what he wants to do." Her man, Jamal, 30, is into what he wants to do, and much of it does not include Trina.

"I've tried to get him to go to church with me on Sunday," Trina added, "but he'd rather play ball with his friends. I am tired of putting up with him. It seems like he cares more for them, than for me. Is he the one or not?"

◌ Diagnosis ◌

I told Trina, "Actions speak louder than words. Your man's actions are telling you that he does not want to be your man, but you are trying not to hear it. He is a constant disappearing act, and his actions are trying to give you serious clues that he is not the one. You appear to be receiving the crumbs of this relationship while he is getting the cake. Do you deserve a life of crumbs? Do you enjoy being the last priority in his life? If the answer to those questions is no, then do something about it," I challenged her.

"Jamal seems to have an adolescent mind-set. Dating an immature person is hard work. It's like dating and raising them at the same time. It is not worth the effort, because those you have to raise rarely appreciate your sacrifices. You are compromising your faith with this activity."

It is risky to love someone who does not want you. The wrong one can damage your self-esteem and destroy you, mentally and emotionally. I've seen women who desperately held on to the wrong men, but in the end they were angry, bitter, frustrated. A man like Jamal is unlikely to change.

Women need to pay attention to their man's behavior. A man who will not go to church with you automatically disqualifies himself. It's a natural screening process. If he won't go with you, then you can't be with him, period. Church attendance is non-negotiable. I'm not suggesting that churchgoers are perfect.

No, they can lie and cheat, too. The difference is that the man who goes to church is at least willing to sit in the presence of God with you. This lessens his chances of being worthless.

∽ **Prescription** ∽

I advised Trina to get rid of Jamal. "But end it with class. Be the better person than him from beginning to end. One of the keys to ending a negative relationship is understanding that you can survive by yourself," I said. Being by yourself does not dictate loneliness, just as having someone does not guarantee joy. You need a mentor and a set of girlfriends who are about something other than chasing silly men. Find a church that has a progressive singles ministry. There you will find like-minded men and women. Set some boundaries regarding what you will and will not accept. Stop settling for whatever.

You have the right to be happy. Let me share with you a personal bill of rights:

- I have numerous choices in my life beyond mere survival.

- I have a right to follow my own values and standards.

- I have a right to dignity and respect.

- I have a right to express myself as long as I am not abusive to others.

- I have a right to all my feelings.

- I have a right to determine and honor my own priorities.

- I have a right to say no when I feel I am not ready, its unsafe, or violates my values.

• I have a right to be uniquely me, without feeling I'm not good enough.[1]

∞ **Case 2** ∞

Jason, a 33-year-old photographer, offered another concern. "I love my lady. We've been together for three years, but she has her ways," he said. "She is jealous. I mean real jealous and I can't understand why." Jason's lady is an aggressive, angry woman. The fact that she looks like a combination of Halle Berry and Vivica Fox and Janet Jackson causes Jason not to fret too much about her behavior. "Her looks make up for a lot," he reasoned.

He met his lady at his church. She is the preacher's daughter. When she's not in one of her jealous moods, she is an upstanding Christian woman. The notion of marrying her and becoming a part of the first family also appeals to Jason.

"I give her my time, my love, even my money. But she still thinks that I am up to something. If we are in the store and I greet the checkout clerk, she thinks I am being flirty. She watches my eyes to see if I am looking at women who walk past. I have done everything she asks of me, and it is still not enough. This ain't right, is it?" Jason asked.

∞ **Diagnosis** ∞

"Jason," I said, "you are in love with a dangerous person. The longer that you stay with her, the more control she will exercise in your life. Do you honestly think that it is normal, natural, or desirable to have someone monitor who you look at? It is not. This relationship is not normal, it is dangerous. Men sometimes underestimate the potential for harm that can come from a possessive woman. There are reasons to be concerned. Your self-worth, your health, your life is at stake.

"She may be all that, but she is also more of a hassle to deal with emotionally. No sane person wants to be controlled and manipulated the way she does you. A three-year relationship is not easy to toss away," I added.

"And without question there is an allure to being a part of the first family of your church. Many churches put the pastor and family up on a pedestal. I appreciate your interest in joining that. But what would it be like to be there, in the spotlight, and be married to a woman who makes you sick?"

∞ Prescription ∞

I told Jason that he must move beyond the visual in his relationships. What you see is not always what you get. All that glitters is not gold. Men must learn the value of protecting their hearts. They make the mistake of feeling invincible. Also they can make the mistake of not feeling anything. It's called being cool. Coolness keeps men silent in the face of danger. Coolness keeps men from thinking out the consequence of their actions. They believe that if they pause to reflect, they will be derided.

"Run, Jason, run," I ordered. "Don't be afraid to end it. It's perfectly OK to stop what is not right. Sometimes men are suckered into believing that they prove their manhood by staying in difficult situations. Look, Jesus already went to the cross, he suffered the sins of the world. There is no need for you to take on this unnecessary suffering. Jesus already paid the price."

Making tough decisions is necessary in the game of love. This Love Clinic showed us that negative relationships are ungodly. We deserve the best and must never settle for less. We ended this session on a high note of hope for singles. We don't want them to give up on love, just be careful in the pursuit of love. They need the love of God to do what they have to do in the love department. Encouragement came from Isaiah 40:30–31: *Though youths grow weary and tired, And vigorous young men stumble badly, Yet those who wait for the Lord will gain strength; They will mount up with wings like eagles, They will run and not get tired, They will walk and not become weary.*

Let us pray

Dear God,

Loving You means loving ourselves. That's how to stop the madness. When relationships are wrong, open our mouths to speak what must be said. Let our faith in You be reflected in the way we let others treat us. Give us the courage to do what is right.

Amen

Chapter 5

HOW LONG MUST I WAIT?

They say that patience is a virtue, but when a brother or a sister is waiting on the Lord to send them a mate, patience is over-rated. Nobody likes to wait. We live in a hurry-up society. We are accustomed to having what we want, when we want it, where we want it. The problems come when we try to apply the instant gratification philosophy to finding a mate.

Christian folk know how to quote all the right scriptures about waiting: *Those who wait for the Lord . . . will mount up with wings like eagles* (Isaiah 40:31). But the truth is waiting makes us stressed out and strained. It's times like these when our faith must move into high gear. The wait is like a Christian exercise that helps us to develop muscles called patience, hope, and perseverance.

∽ Case 1 ∽

The first sister who approached the microphone brought her diary with her. She clutched it so tightly that initially I thought it was her Bible. Her name was Vivian; she was 42 years old and had been waiting on God for some time. "I wanted to be one of the first to speak tonight, because I want to set the tone for tonight on joy. If we keep on worrying about what we don't have, we will wind up with nothing," she said.

Vivian has never been married. She is active in her church and leads one of the singles ministries in the city. The more she talked, the clearer it became why she was so happy. "I have not always been so patient," she continued. "Over the years, I've watched my other girlfriends stroll down the aisle. But it was never my turn. I kept asking God when do I stroll, when do I stroll? And God said wait. Well, I got tired of waiting and I decided to go and find a man on my own terms. That was a huge mistake. I wound up with a guy who I quickly determined was not for me. The only problem was that he did not agree with my assessment. He kept calling me and hanging out at my job and my house. Finally I got a police protective order against him. He is gone now, but the lesson is clear. Unless God sends him I do not want him," she stressed.

Vivian had one more thing to tell us. She opened her diary and began to read. "Lord, it's around midnight, it's raining outside and dark and cozy in here, you know what I'd rather be doing now. My body is talking to me and it is saying go and get a man. But Lord, you have given me power before to be strong and wait. I need a big dose *right now*. I believe all that God has for me. But I have one question—are women supposed to sit around and wait? Or do we have any say in the matter? And if I do, how do I avoid any more stalkers?"

∽ Diagnosis ∾

Sometimes our situations look like nightmares, but God uses the darkness to see if we will keep on walking. Just being able to put one foot in front of the other shows God that we are serious about Him and His role in our lives. Many people needed to hear Vivian's story. Her struggles with waiting are proof that our God will make a way somehow. When a woman is 40 years old and not married, people look at her funny. They say, "Baby, why aren't you married yet? Is anything wrong?" They don't understand that God has your situation already designed and figured out. All you have to do is walk in it and on his word.

I told Vivian, "Your diary sounds like it is an essential part of your life. It is great to have an outlet like that. Sometimes just writing something down on paper can make us feel better. If more of us could find healthy outlets for our concerns and problems we could reduce the power and potential of their threat. Our negatives only tend to multiply when we give them too much attention."

∽ Prescription ∾

Let me address the concern regarding finding a man. Many people cite Proverbs 18:22 as the lone voice regarding women and men looking for each other: *He who finds a wife, finds a good thing And obtains favor from the Lord.* This passage endorses the process of men locating outstanding women to be their wives. Yet this passage does not exclude women from looking for a man either. God does not want single women sitting at home expecting their future husbands to come and knock on the door. God wants women to see what is out there and what is available for them.

What we don't want is to see women moving into a hyper-aggressive mode where they snatch men off the streets. There has to be a balance in the process. God gives us the spirit of discernment, which means that with God's help we can determine whether people mean us good or bad. Looking does not mean not waiting. The two go hand in hand. And as you look don't forget about what is known as the "overlooked brother."[1] These steady, reliable, hardworking men are often overlooked in our search for the six-figure man with the six-pack, driving the Mercedes. Here is a partial list of places you can find the overlooked brother. Good luck.

1. Church

2. Conventions of fraternal organizations

3. Religious conventions

4. Music festivals

5. Street fairs

6. Volunteer activities

7. Special interest stores

8. YMCA

9. Tennis clubs

10. Laundromats[2]

∞ Case 2 ∞

Men are struggling with the burden of waiting as well. They may not articulate the intense degree of their pain, but it is there. Maybe they are more patient than women. Maybe the gender imbalance that makes them outnumbered by women by the millions gives them a quiet confidence that they will meet their queen.

Malik, 33, had been blessed with money. When a young man has in his possession that much cash, trouble can't be too far away. "My money made me a fool," he said candidly. "I knew that I was to wait on the Lord for a sign about the women that I was seeing, but the only sign that I saw was a green light. The honeys must have seen the same light, because they were buzzing all around.

"The trouble that I fell into was that I rushed into relationships without any thought or any prayer. I was high on my money. I thought that money would be the great cure for what ailed me. I thought that I could buy the woman of my dreams, and that everything would work out fine. Rushing and waiting was a stupid combination. It brought me women from hell. They were out for my money. They did not care about me. They were self-centered and egotistical. When a brother is out there on his own, he is in trouble," Malik said. "My question now is how do I get back in with God?"

∽ **Diagnosis** ∾

People think that waiting on the Lord is a woman's issue. They are wrong. Men need to wait on the Lord, too. Their physical strength deceives them and makes them think they are greater than they are. In Malik's case, his financial blessings made him think that he had it going on more than he really did. The money gave him a mental rush, and he rushed on ahead of God. As he relied more on the dollars, he took his eyes off of the provider of the dollars. That's where he went wrong.

The women that he hooked up with are exactly what we get when we press on without God. We get the bad attitudes and gold-digging ways that make us run back to find God.

∽ **Prescription** ∾

"After the experiences that you've had you came back to God and said that you'll gladly wait on the right one. Don't feel too bad—it happens to the best of us. The Good News is that you are able to come home again," I said. "All of us can come home to God again, no matter what we have done. There was another young man, much like yourself who came into a large sum of money. The money made him rush into things too. He left home, partied, and hung out with all types of people. But when his money ran out, the party people left too. The young man became destitute and had to work on a pig farm. Can you imagine that fall? He went from being the wealthy uttermost, to becoming the pig farm gutter-most. While at his job at the pig farm, he realized that he did not have to live like that because his father had a comfortable home. But he worried that his dad might not welcome him home. The young man went home anyway, and when he was just a few feet away from the house, his dad saw him and rushed out to welcome him. That's the biblical saga of the Prodigal Son.

"Malik, the Lord is rushing out to meet you right now. The fact that you left home, turned your back on God, and sinned does not matter now. What matters is that you have come home. Let God restore you in the places that were torn down during your wild times. God wants to revive your spirit so that you will have a close relationship with him. When God gets done with you, waiting will be an easy task, because you are confident that God has what you need."

We closed this session by reading about the power of God to sustain us no matter what, as found in Philippians 4: 11–13:

Not that I speak from want, for I have learned to be content in whatever circumstances I am. I know how to get along with humble means, and I also know how to live in prosperity; in any and every circumstance I have learned the secret of being filled and going hungry, both of having abundance and suffering need. I can do all things through Him who strengthens me.

Let us pray
Dear God,
Thank you for the victory in waiting. Thank you for the spirit of calm and peace that you are flooding me with right now. Thank you in advance for the mate that you have for me. You are a good God; there is no failure in you.
Amen

Chapter 6

YOU'RE NEVER TOO OLD FOR LOVE

Don't snicker at the grayheaded couple holding hands as they stroll down the street. Senior love should be respected and even admired. The mere fact that they are old *and* in love is a goal we should all be striving for. "Life revolves around relationships, and it shows in aging. People who maintain close relationships live longer and are healthier."[1] We are never too old for love. Some erroneously relegate mature persons to rocking chairs and walking canes, believing that only the young, with their vim and vigor, are able to access passion. Many senior citizens refuse to be locked out of the love department.

Older couples can take us to school. According to a study in *The Journal of Psychology and Aging*, older couples can settle their differences with less stress than younger couples. They are less angry, disgusted, belligerent, and whiny with each other than younger couples.[2] Specifically, the study lists four key traits of successful older couples. First, they maintain a strong sense of commitment. They don't threaten separation or divorce as a result of a disagreement. Second, they share their feelings with their partner to maintain intimacy. They grow closer over the years. This is especially important in the area of sexual relations. Third, they have developed a friendship with each other. This enables them to be good companions. Fourth, they are flexible. They were able to adapt to stress and change. The couples who were flexible fought less.[3]

There's a good chance that many of us will see old age, because life expectancy has increased. The Scriptures confirm that age is just a number. They tell us in Psalm 92:14, *They will still yield fruit in old age; they shall be full of sap and very green.* There is a smile on Deacon McClain's face during worship that has nothing to do with the sermon. His wife, Sarah, nuzzled beside him has just whispered something romantic in his ear, and he can't wait to get home. Fellow churchgoers don't understand that love and passion can live on in the lives of older saints. Studies tell us that the majority of persons past age 65 continue to have both interest in and capacity for sexual relations. "This capacity for satisfying sexual relations continues into the 70s and 80s for healthy couples."[4]

Seniors in love can be considered a strange topic. Our society is fixated on brand new. If it's not young and fresh, nobody wants it. Elderly people are considered sick, weak, and in the way. That attitude is called ageism and ageism, like racism and sexism and all the other "isms," is a sin. Ageism stems from our fear of growing old. "When old age is perceived as something undesirable and miserable, then those who fear becoming old distance themselves from those who already have the disease."[5] The Bible teaches us that God never forsakes the elderly, and we should not either: *I have been young and now I am old, yet I have not seen the righteous forsaken or his descendants begging bread* (Psalm 37:25).

Seasoned citizens have feelings that are flowing, and it is time for the church to recognize and appreciate venerable love. God's gift of love has no age limit attached.

∽ Case 1 ∾

Leroy and Lola are a phenomenal couple of 80-year-old newlyweds. Frail yet feisty, they offered a powerful testimony about attraction, love, and the aged. "We just got married," he said. "It's been about six weeks now. I think marriage is a good thing at any age. It's been good for me thus far." Both Leroy and Lola experienced the death of their spouses, but they did not hesitate to embrace love when it came around again.

Both were widowed, lonely, and not ashamed to do something about it. The new groom explained it matter-of-factly, "I was lonely and needed a roommate, and there she was. I'd seen her up at the store, and I felt like she'd be good for me. There is no sense just sitting around, when you want to be with someone," said Leroy. "I asked her if she'd be my wife, and she said sure."

The spry twosome indicated that initially their families were not very happy about their relationship. "My daughters had a natural fit," Lola shared. "They claimed that I was too old to have a boyfriend, and too old to have feelings like that. They must have thought I was already dead, huh? His kids didn't like it either, but we are still the parents, and what we say goes."

"A few of our children are still worked up about it. But our love is here to stay." Leroy laughed.

∽ Diagnosis ∾

I told them, "Leroy and Lola, your love is a beacon of hope for so many of us. Someone right now feels as if they will never have love in their life. And they hear how God has blessed in your situation. Thank you for sharing with us. You show us that our ability to be attractive or pursue attractiveness in the love department does not diminish with age. We certainly ought to give God some praise for your love.

"The initial discouragement you received from your children is not surprising," I continued. "Our children, no matter what their age, will always be our children. Perhaps they were troubled by the fact that you found someone new because it seemed like a betrayal of their deceased parent. They had an image of you two with your first spouses, and it is difficult for them to change.

"Also they could be dealing with basic separation issues where the boundaries between them and you as parents were never established," I said.

> Parents become so wrapped up in the lives of their children that they vicariously live through them . . . Such parents cannot allow their children to become adults and cannot give up the role of parenting. In turn the children, even up to middle age, cannot let go of the parents.[6]

∽ Prescription ∾

When seniors want to connect with a partner and children stand in the way, I suggest that you lay down the law. Go old school on them and show them who is boss. Have a family conference and explain to the children once and for all that the marriage is to be taken seriously and respected. As parents age, their children occasionally feel that they are in control. Don't allow the displeasure of the others to rain on your love parade. Treasure each other and each day that the Lord gives you. Continue to act as role models for love for the rest of us.

⚬ Case 2 ⚬

Some seniors are still looking for love. One single sister, Odessa, a 66-year-old retired teacher with a head of regal gray hair, said, "I've been married twice. I have two grown children, but both of them are hooked on crack and I am raising their children. My health has been up and down because I'm a diabetic. Is it too much to ask for the company of a man?" The trials and tribulations of her life would make anyone question whether God had run out of blessings with her name on them.

Odessa's request for a man was legitimate, but the numbers are not in her favor. Women live longer than men: "Among folks over 65, 48 percent are widows, 14 percent are widowers. There are more older women than older men, and more older single women than older single men."[7]

"I was in a lot of pain and depressed for a long time. Then God spoke to my heart and encouraged me to quit crying and take a different look at life. Sure I was alone," she continued. "But I did not have to be lonely. Most of all, there was a possibility that God had someone for me. All I had to do was open my eyes," she said.

∽ Diagnosis ∾

"Sister Odessa, I am glad that you came out tonight," I told her, "because God wanted you to be in the right place to hear these words about your situation. It is normal to be discouraged about life. Your family situation is challenging to you. I can see the sorrow you have with your older children, yet there is joy with your grandchildren. Your health is also an issue. Don't let that diabetes get the best of you. Please eat right and get plenty of exercise.

"As a result of all that you are going through," I continued, "I believe that you are in the midst of what is known as the 'Mara mentality.'[8] In the Book of Ruth we meet Ruth's mother-in-law Naomi. Naomi encountered a series of difficulties in her life. Her husband and son both died. As a result of the tragedies, she said to them, *'Do not call me Naomi; call me Mara, for the Almighty has dealt very bitterly with me'* (Ruth 1:20). The Mara mentality will keep you looking at what is going wrong in your life instead of what is going right."

∽ Prescription ∾

When people reach a certain age they will probably have seen a collection of tragedies. Discouragement comes when people think they have seen it all and most of it was terrible! But no matter what age you are, you have not seen it all. "There are no graduations from the school of life other than death. No one knows how God will end His book, but He does save the best for last."[9]

Hold on, your best days are yet to come. Let me leave with

a poem written by another single senior sister, entitled "Love in the Winter of Life."

> I like to think of love in the golden age
> some say it's impossible and they go into a rage,
> our hair may be white but our souls are at ease,
> but we are at liberty to fall in love, if we please.
>
> We may be bereft of our former mate
> that doesn't mean that we can never date
> sometimes it's done for many a good reason
> Love in the Winter of Life is yet another season.

Poem reprinted with permission of Charlie Mae Heggens.

We closed this session by celebrating God's good gift of longevity. We read in Leviticus 19:32, *"You shall rise up before the grayheaded and honor the aged, and you shall revere your God; I am the Lord."*

Let us pray
   Dear God,
   Thank You for the ability to love. You've poured out Your spirit into our bodies and we use them to show forth who You are. Our relationships are testimony to Your love that changes not. You have kept us and never left us. We praise You for the consistency of being cared for throughout our lives. Open our hearts to the affections You place before us.
   Amen

Chapter 7

TO SHACK OR NOT TO SHACK?

Every saint has a past and every sinner has a future. If communion rails and altar steps could talk, they would tell us the confessions of church-folk living in sin. Cohabitation, or shacking, is one of the biggest secrets of churches. It is there, but few people talk about it publicly. It is only whispered that Brother John and Sister Sally share the same address. It is inferred that Tasha's boyfriend lives with her. We look the other way and pretend it is not going on. Yet cohabitation is real. According to the latest statistics some 3.3 million households in America are cohabituated.[1] This figure is up by 72 percent according to the latest census figures.[2]

Living together is not a good idea, or a godly one either. Biblically, men and women who seek a committed relationship are instructed to marry. This creates a spiritual bond between the couple and God. That's what the Scripture means by *and the two shall become one flesh* (Ephesians 5:31.) Without the Lord in the midst of the relationship, it is doomed from the start.

Couples fall into the shacking trap for a number of reasons. Past issues, fear of commitment, escape from the restrictions of a formal marriage, sex on a regular basis, and flexibility all lead to cohabitating without marriage. A pretend marriage doesn't lock anyone in. If it works, it works. If it does not, it does not. They can easily go their separate ways. The attitude of no harm done is not right or healthy. When people who are living together break up, it is often with even greater uproar because of unhealthy attachments and feelings. Finances can be strained if the couple has merged bank accounts or purchased major ticket items together such as a house, car, household appliances, and credit cards. And if children are a part of the union, troubles are a certainty.

Statistics tell us that "the divorce rate is higher, about 50 percent higher—among people who live together before they marry."[3] Cohabitants don't have the faith in God or in relationships. They all seem to be running from something.

∽ Case 1 ∾

Jimmy and Jasmine were two graduate students who had lived together for about one year before the Lord turned their lives and their love around. Their tumultuous relationship had highs, like reciting love poetry at coffeehouses around campus, and dramatic lows, like throwing plates at each other. They met at an on-campus party, had sex that same night, and had been together ever since.

"Our personalities clicked when we met that night," explained Jimmy, who with his thick glasses and khakis looked very academic. "She was on the dance floor grooving to the beat and I said 'whoa, I've got to have her.' I stepped to her and the rest is history. She looked good and that was all that mattered to me. Getting married was the last thing on my mind," he added.

Jimmy was the first of his family to attend college. While he was proud of the achievement, he was weary of the pressure. Academic excellence came easy for him, so he was able to invest a sizeable portion of his time in the pursuit of social events. To him, Jasmine was a social event. She was a good time, plain and simple. He was in grad school to get a degree, not a wife.

"We come from broken families," Jimmy explained. "As kids, Jasmine and I saw marriages that were painful and difficult. Divorce hurt our parents and it hurt us too. We had no faith in the whole marriage thing. That's what brought us together. But it wasn't enough to keep us together. Even though the sex was great, the other parts of the relationship were not so great. The longer we were together, the meaner Jasmine got. We fought a lot, and I stayed at the library longer so I wouldn't have to put up with her back at the apartment. The strange part was that as bad as it was, I still could not leave," he said.

Jasmine, a tall, studious sister with a short haircut, jumped in the conversation: "Yeah, I was hard to deal with because I wanted to get married. I knew Jimmy was a good catch. An educated brother, working on a Master's degree? Please! I was after him like he was after me. He was looking for fun. I was looking for future," she explained. "I kept telling him that I loved him, but he never responded. That made me boiling mad, but I stayed."

Jasmine had a high IQ, but low self-esteem. Although she

had been awarded a full academic scholarship and a veritable guarantee of a highly paid position with a national firm, Jasmine's insecurity undercut her accomplishments like a knife. Growing up an only child with her mom, a single parent, Jasmine vowed that whenever she came within striking distance of a good man she would go for it. And Jimmy was her target.

Jimmy and Jasmine's live-in relationship came to a head one Easter Sunday when the couple decided to attend a church near the campus. The pastor's sermon convicted their hearts of the sin that they were living in, and before they knew it, they were walking down the aisle to join the church.

Unbeknownst to the couple, the church they had joined was theologically conservative and did not accept members into the flock who were living together but were not married. They were motivated by the eloquent speech of the pastor, the swelling crowd in attendance, and the dazzling edifice. The two had not taken the time to research this church's theological positions.

"I thought that joining the church would help us make sense of what we were doing. Something about the relationship didn't feel right," Jimmy reflected. "I now know that it was the guilt I was feeling swirling around inside me."

"As soon as we completed the membership forms after service, they saw the same address and told us, 'Look, God does not approve of what you're doing. It's time to get right," Jasmine recalled. "They prayed with us, laid hands on us, and some of them spoke in tongues. When they were done, we were not the same."

Jimmy added, "I've moved out of her place and into my own, and we are seeing each other in class or on weekend dates. No more sleeping together. No more fights, no more tension. Everything is a lot more calm and our grades are better. What is the next step for us?"

∽ Diagnosis ∽

I praise God that these two were delivered from cohabitation. The year that they spent together brought out the worst in them because it was the worst kind of relationship. Actions and activities that are outside the will of God cannot benefit us. The fact that each of them wanted to end the relationship but could not indicates that the both of them were tied to each other. It sounds like they are dealing with "soul ties." This is a spiritual condition in which the very souls of two people are linked or tied and is best known to be the consequence of sex before marriage. The primary symptom of soul ties is an overwhelming desire to be with someone who you really can't stand. When you are around them, they make you sick, yet you are drawn to them. It does not even matter if they mistreat you, being with them is all that matters.

In the Book of Genesis 34 we see the effect of soul ties in a young couple, Dinah and Sechem. We are told that *he lay with her by force* (34: 2–3). Even though mutual love was not a part of the relationship, the act of sex served as a cement that locked two people together who would be better off separated. Soul ties keep us revolving in a mess that we need to get out of.

Also, the year of living together immersed them into the "cohabitation factor"—beliefs and behaviors that will diminish the chances of a happy marriage. According to a study from the

University of Wisconsin, there are at least four characteristics of couples who live together:

1. They don't believe that marriage can last forever.

2. They are less enthusiastic about family life.

3. They do not receive the family support that married couples receive.

4. They develop bad relationship habits.[4]

∞ Prescription ∞

"Jimmy and Jasmine you two are caught up in counterfeit relationships," I said. "Such relationships seem real and fulfilling, but they are not. Many individuals don't understand why a certain person has such control over their lives and why they can't forget that person. The bondage caused by counterfeit oneness can make individuals think they can't break up and escape—even when the dating relationship is abusive.[5]

"If you belong to God and are involved in a relationship of counterfeit oneness, you can't expect anything eventually but grief.[6] The fact that you two no longer live together is excellent. It gives you the opportunity to see what your relationship is really made of. You can spend time together to determine if there is any compatibility, or any friendship between the two of you. Couples need more than physical attraction to survive. Couples need the love of Christ. More importantly, the time apart gives you time to reflect and study God's Word. Since you both are excellent students of academia, let's see you apply yourselves to the Scriptures."

Some people believe that it is easy and effortless to achieve a successful marriage. They don't understand that they will need God's help to construct them into people who can sustain a marriage. This will be a lengthy process. "The ability to love your mate, serve, and sacrifice is not a quality God bestows on you the moment you say, 'I do.' You can't learn to sacrifice, serve, or love by taking a course or reading a book. The only way you can develop those qualities is by being in such a close fellowship with God that his love flows through you."[7]

"Jimmy," I said, "the time apart will determine whether or not you can view Jasmine as something other than a sex object. She is more than that," I told him. "Sex has a priority in your life. Sex is a powerful lure. It clouds the mind by overexciting the body. In Matthew 6:22–23 we can read about the clouded spirits: *The eye is the lamp of the body; so then if your eye is clear, your whole body will be full of light. But if your eye is bad, your whole body will be full of darkness.*

"Jasmine, your quest for a husband gave you a lot more than you bargained for. If Jimmy is the right one, let time and the Lord tell you so. In the same book, Matthew 6:25, the Lord tells us that everything is already handled: *For this reason I say to you, do not be worried about your life, as to what you will eat or what you will drink; nor for your body, as to what you will put on. Is not life more than food, and the body than clothing?*"

This young couple appeared to be on the right track to heal from the affects of cohabitation.

∽ Case 2 ∽

Gillian, was the next person to talk about her life as a shacker. She has lived with four different men over a ten-year period, opting never to tie the knot. This somber, 40-ish hairstylist has paid an awful price for her lifestyle. She contracted gonorrhea. The sexually transmitted disease (STD) went untreated for weeks and Gillian came down with pelvic inflammatory disease, which led to her infertility.

In the U.S. alone over one million cases of gonorrhea lead to PID. Tubal damage and scarring will cause 20 percent of women to become infertile, 18 percent to develop chronic pelvic pain, and 9 percent to have ectopic pregnancies.[8]

Gillian said, "I always thought that I would be a mommy someday, but here I am sterile due to my walk on the wild side. I want to testify that living with men is not the way to go. Yes, I was getting it on, but now I've paid the ultimate price. When I was in the midst of it I thought I was being sassy and sophisticated. All my friends were doing it too. It was the thing! But in the end, the guys did not respect me. They ended up leaving me, even though I tried to hang on to them. Of course, my church members did not know. I kept them guessing as to whether or not I even had a man in my life. I hold a high office at church, and I have appearances to think about."

Cohabitation felt natural and comfortable for Gillian because she had experienced it in her childhood. Her mom never married her father, but rather had lived with him and a string of other men over the years.

"I learned early and I learned well that marriage is not worth the paper it is printed on. I learned that men are to be used and tossed away. And I learned that living with a guy is about the best I can do. The all-American family will not happen for me," she said. "I hope that my experiences can keep another person from making the same mistakes that I did. Now that I am on my own I feel so guilty. I feel like God is punishing me. Is the STD God's way of punishing me?" Gillian asked.

❧ Diagnosis ❧

"Gillian, God is not punishing you," I assured her. "You are reaping what you have sown. Our actions have consequences to them. You are paying a very painful cost for living with men. God still loves you and still seeks your best future. But let's face some facts first.

"My sister, you are a serial cohabitator. You've run from man to man to man. All that running has exhausted you. The running shows us that you are commitment phobic—afraid of settling down and opening up your life and your love. Without question what you experienced when you were younger poisoned you to healthy, sustained relationships. It's called a generational stronghold. It's a sin passed on from your mother to you."

A stronghold is "a forceful, stubborn rationale, opinion, idea or philosophy that is formed and resistant to the knowledge of Jesus Christ."[9] Sadly, strongholds are not rare, says family counselor Dr. Clarence Walker. In his book *Breaking Stronghold in the African American Family*, he writes about the generational nature of strongholds:

When a family, a couple, or a people hold on to opinions, behaviors, ideas, and arguments that are contrary to the Word of
God, they become the enemy of God, and therefore, hate God.
The Bible says to love Him is to keep His commandments. The
result is that strongholds can be passed down from one family
generation to another as a legacy, "visiting the iniquity of the
fathers upon the children unto the third and fourth generation
of them that hate me." (Exodus 20:5). As is a mother, so is her
daughter.[10]

∞ Prescription ∞

I advised Gillian that she is in need of a spiritual makeover. The
aspect of her as a single woman in Christ has yet to be culti-
vated. She's always been a woman living with a man, and needs
to discover what her life will be like with Jesus as her man. A
single woman in Christ has many blessings at her fingertips. She
will find peace, and joy in her life.

While a woman is single, she needs to recognize that she has a
unique opportunity to build herself up in the Lord without the
drains that can occur later . . . This time is in your life for you
to charge up your battery cells. It's time to pamper; a time to
take luxurious baths in milk and honey. You can lie there in the
bath and worship the Lord. It's a ministry you have. So before
you ask God for another man, take care of Him. If you are not
ministering to His needs and are before Him asking Him to give
you one of his princes to minister to, your prayers are not being
heard, because you are not ministering to Him.[11]

We ended this Love Clinic by celebrating our creation as holy temples designed by God. We recited 1 Corinthians 6:19–20: *Or do you not know that your body is a temple of the Holy Spirit who is in you, whom you have from God, and that you are not your own? For you have been bought with a price: therefore glorify God in your body.*

Let us pray

Dear God,

We praise You for the spirit of perseverance. You are able to help us overcome. We need Your strength. We need Your power to hold out. Come Holy Spirit, come heavenly dove. Amen

Chapter 8

BEFORE YOU SAY "I DO"

Engaged couples desperately need sound premarital advice, and ironically, churches can be the last place for it. Many pastors offer a wink, a nod, and do what comes naturally as their advice to the newlywed couple as they exit the sanctuary after the wedding. Due to this dearth of pastoral guidance, hellish households and gruesome twosomes exist in church congregations. The problem stems from the reluctance to discuss relationships and the mechanics of marriage. Over time, the close-knit nature of the church community has unraveled, family support has evaporated, and valuable information has not been passed on to the next generation. Misinformation, rumors, and innuendo have become commonplace. People had no idea what they were getting into, or what to do when they got there.

Love makes people drunk. Love is intoxicating. Lovers are head over heels with giggles and grins. Love and romance can bring sweaty palms, racing heartbeats and butterflies in the stomach.

> When you meet a strong candidate for love, your limbic system is flooded with a powerful concoction—so powerful that scientists believe it is an . . . altered state of consciousness. It is induced by the action of phenyl ethylamine (PEA), which is a naturally occurring, amphetamine-like neuro-transmitter. PEA, known as the love molecule, works in concert with dopamine and norepinephrine and triggers incredible side effects. Symptoms include a delightfully positive attitude, increased energy, decreased need for sleep, and loss of appetite.[1]

Sometimes in the lovey-dovey stage before marriage we put on rose-colored glasses and only see what we want to see. We see habits, traits, and mannerisms as cute, different, or attractive. Maybe he stutters when he is nervous or maybe her fork always finds its way over to his plate. But once the vows are taken and we experience those habits on a daily basis, they can become a nuisance. Larger issues can strike at the heart of a marriage as well. Engaged couples are high on each other and can make errors in judgment just like those high on drugs. Premarital counseling sobers them up to face their future.

Jack and Jill want to get married *now*. Their church has a lengthy period of time couples must wait before marriage, and requires premarital classes. Jack and Jill decide they know best. After all, they reason, how much can a class teach them about each other? So, in their blissful ignorance, they elope. What Jack does not know is that Jill plans to get pregnant as soon as possible, have at least five children, and become a stay-at-home mom for the next 20 years. Jack does not know this because he and Jill have never discussed the details of marriage. There was no need to, they are in love. What Jill does not know is that Jack wants a wife with a career, and he does not want any children at all. In fact, he has had a vasectomy. Jill does not know this because Jack is uncomfortable discussing his past. Jill and Jack never discussed the details of what their life will be like as a married couple. After all, they are in love.

Love is not enough to maintain a happy marriage. Engaged couples need to spend quality time getting to know each other beyond the notions of favorite color or foods. Only a trained counselor can provide the in-depth probing that effectively reveals couples' similarities and differences. Premarital counseling gives engaged couples a new and necessary perspective on each other and on their hopes and dreams for the future. Those who proceed without it may needlessly experience choppy waters. I keep a full premarital counseling roster because I love it. The preventive work of love is so much more pleasant than the emergency intervention. In my premarital sessions we cover the main areas of concern for couples: in-laws, money, communication, sex, household duties, child-rearing, jobs, and future plans. No topic is too small or insignificant. It is amazing how couples come into the session assuming that they know their loved one completely. Once I probe, pull, and push, they see and hear a different person. That's not because someone was intentionally withholding the truth, but because all of us have unspoken expectations. When we are blissfully in love, we think the other person knows what our expectations are. We are wrong.

Premarital counseling is a powerful tool. Marriage is too important to mess up with rushed, half-stepping acts. If you value yourself and the one you seek to marry, you will pause, look, listen and learn all you can about that person before you say "I do."

∞ Case 1 ∞

Nicole and Bruce, both 28-year-old postal workers, came forward to share their concerns. They had been dating about a year and wanted to marry, but there was a major roadblock to cross before they could truly become one flesh. Bruce refused to go one step further until this issue was resolved.

Nicole had never cut the apron strings. In fact, she shared an apartment and a car with her mom. Nicole's mother and father had never married, so Nicole and her mom grew up together. A fifteen-year age difference between them made them even closer, and Nicole's mom wanted to make up for the lack of a father by holding on tight to her baby girl. This mother-daughter duo developed a tightly bound relationship that threatened to choke the life out of Nicole's impending marriage.

"Plain and simple her mom did not want me around," Bruce said. "She was nice while we were just dating, but once we started to get serious, I saw another side of her. She copped an attitude with me. I felt like I was breaking up a home or something. If I phoned their apartment, sometimes she would not let me speak to Nicole. She'd talk to me all crazy. I did not know what to do because Nicole was in denial."

Nicole was so close to the situation that she could not see her mother's negative influence on her relationship with Bruce and what a potential menace Nicole's mom was to her future happiness.

"I knew I was in love with him the first time I saw him at church," Nicole said breathlessly. "I set aside time and energy to communicate with God. I'd been praying, fasting, and seeking the Lord that he might send me a husband. And there he was. Mom was sitting with me when I saw him and she thought he was nice too. She's got her ways. She is Mom.

"I think that Bruce is overreacting because he and his family are not as close as mine," Nicole added. "He barely speaks to his mother once a week. That is not good either. Parents and their kids should be together. He is getting on my nerves hounding me about my mother. She has been with me longer than him. Blood is thicker than water. Don't force me to make an easy choice between the two of you. The Bible does say honor thy father and thy mother. I am just doing God's will," she said, snapping her head for emphasis.

∽ Diagnosis ∾

While it is not uncommon for adult children and their parents to have involved, loving relationships, the relationship between Nicole and her mom is more like lockdown. Nicole does not seem to feel the pressure of the handcuffs. It is of concern to me that she is comfortable with the restrictions and possessive behavior. Nicole's mom has parented her the best way she knows how, but she needs to realize it's time to let go.

"Nicole, you and your mom have some deep emotional involvement," I said. "From what I've heard, it sounds unhealthy. It sounds like she sees you as a possession. She is not prepared to let you go, because for so long you belonged to her and she belonged to you. You two were in an exclusive relationship.

Right now, you are bearing the brunt of dysfunctional parenting. She loves you, but her love is crippling because it won't let you fly free. Those things in life that we love, we must offer the freedom to leave if they like. You've only known constriction and it feels safe. But is it not normal.

"Most adults move through three stages of relationship to their parents—from dependence in childhood, to independence as adolescents, and finally to interdependence and cooperation, as between equals, in adulthood.[2]

"You cannot have both the excessive emotional bond with your mother and a marital relationship to Bruce. Nicole, you love your mother, and I hope that never changes, but I want you to understand what her situation as a young single mom was like. Her life impacts you and your upcoming marriage in ways you cannot see. Writer bell hooks writes compellingly about the bravery and brutality of single motherhood. While she does praise those single mothers who soar despite the odds, she admits that 'a poor isolated single female who is not yet emotionally mature, who has not known love, who does not know how to give love to herself or others, will not parent well.'[3]

"Bruce's love challenges all that you've known. He offers you the love of a man. And if you are able to break away from your mother, you can accept his offer," I told her.

I told him, "Bruce, you were wise to slow the process down in order to shed light on this problem. The question that you must ponder now is, do you believe Nicole can change? Most importantly, if she does not change, are you prepared to remain in the marriage? I want you to enter the marriage aware of what may or may not happen. You don't need any surprises."

☙ Prescription ❧

Ephesians 5:31 tells us, *For this reason a man shall leave his father and mother and shall be joined to his wife, and the two shall become one flesh*. While marriage does mean the joining of two people, their families join, too. Healthy, wise couples must create well-defined boundaries with the families before and during the marriage if there is to be peace. Parents need to know their limits; they often need to be reminded of these limits over and over. Some parents are well meaning, just overbearing. Others are controlling and manipulative and seek to render harm.

The Ephesians passage tells us that leaving your parents is respecting them but firmly setting your boundaries. Nicole needs to reshape and redefine her relationship with her mother. Bruce needs to be confident that Nicole is on his side. This couple needs to work on establishing "we-ness" in their relationship, which will point them in a new united direction. We-ness is solidarity between husband and wife. In this case, Nicole will have to side with her husband against her mother. Although this may sound harsh, remember that one of the basic tasks of a marriage is to establish a sense of we-ness between husband and wife.[4]

Nicole must let her mother know that her husband comes first. This will hurt feelings and may even raise some hell, but it must be done. Do it with respect, but with confidence. Marriage is a new life as a team. "For this reason creating or renewing your sense of solidarity with your spouse may involve some rending and tearing away from your primary families."[5]

∽ Case 2 ∾

Adrienne and Roger have been engaged for two years and want to marry. However, they have not married because they are unable to find a point of resolution regarding how to join their households together without causing pain for the children. Adrienne and Roger are both divorced and between them have five children under the age of sixteen. They felt that their divorces traumatized the kids, and did not want to inflict more pain. They had strong faith lives and were active in two separate churches. They brought urgent concerns to premarital counseling and both were open to making the necessary changes to ensure a successful transition. To add to their challenges, they recently discovered they have another baby on the way. While more than 1,300 stepfamilies are created in the United States every day, each family must find its own way.[6]

∽ Diagnosis ∾

It is very wise to consider the children, but do not let them dictate the direction of the marriage. Divorce usually upsets children and remarriage can be equally confusing and confounding.

> A factor that many people in stepfamilies fail to understand is that children, while longing for the home life they once shared with both parents, hate to give up the new friendship they have developed with their parents following the divorce or death. When parents marry someone else, it seems to children that they lost both their former family and their closest friends. In a way they have.[7]

Children of divorce also are forced to give up the notion that their parents will reunite.

Another point of drama with your children may be that they are troubled by the notion that their parents are sexual beings. A new marriage puts you both in a new light in their eyes. They see that you are desirable to the opposite sex. That's a big deal for them. "They are probably going to have difficulty for some time even with displays of affection in their presence."[8]

If Roger is feeling trapped or betrayed by the new pregnancy, feelings of resentment will probably intensify later. Parents have to be careful not to let negative feelings spill over onto the newborn children or the other children.

∞ Prescription ∞

Roger and Adrienne will have to work extra hard to make a smooth transition for the five children. The children will need to feel that their parents love them as well as each other. They will feel lost and alone. Parents can create the harmony that they need. It will be rocky for a while, but one method of transitioning from a single-parent home to a two-parent home is to allow both parents to spend time alone with the children.

Many children have expressed the concern that after their mother or father married again, they spent no time alone with the biological parent. During the time of single parenting, there is usually a great amount of time spent alone with the children. After the remarriage, this interaction often drops immediately to almost none.[9]

Roger and Adrienne must also portray a united front regarding the new baby. The children need to know about the pregnancy—what's going on, and how it impacts their place in the new family unit. The new baby is already creating conflict between them. I suggested that the two marry as soon as possible.

It is often helpful in blended families to involve the children in the ceremony so they feel part of the vows and marriage union. I gave Roger and Adrienne an example of how I'd include the children in their ceremony:

Both of you [names] enter this marriage with children: [list children's names]. These children will have a profound effect on your marriage. It is only with much patience, considerable effort, and a lot of love that this family is going to become what you desire. The commitment you make here is not only a commitment to each other; it is a commitment to each of the children as well.

To the children, let me say that this marriage will have an effect upon each of you as well. You can either view it as gaining another important adult person in your life with whom to share many things or you can see it as an unwelcome intrusion. However, you are part of this family, and families function best when everyone works together. I urge you, therefore, to commit yourselves to this new family, as [couple's names] commit themselves to each other and to you, and may the Lord God bless you all.[10]

We concluded this session with joy as we celebrated the everlasting love of God: *"I have loved you with an everlasting love"* (Jeremiah 31:3).

Let us pray

Dear Lord,

We value marriage, so we protect it. Give engaged couples the bravery to become vulnerable to You and to each other. Bind them together in their surrender and trust. Bless their sincere attempts to become one in Your name.

Amen

Chapter 9

I DON'T LOVE YOU ANYMORE

Dumped, dissed, and dismissed. It is over. The love of your life has kicked you to the curb and you are eating cement. Whether they called it quits by phone or e-mail, or you heard it through the grapevine, it hurts! Life has cruel twists and turns. It seems that your heart is just the latest fatality. Can life get any worse? No. This tops the rip in your trousers, losing your wallet, and missing the subway to work. Can you go on living without that special one? The one who made your heart skip a beat? The one you dreamed of building a life with together? The one you could talk to about anything? Is there anybody else out there like this? The condition of the heart after a breakup is fragile. Just how bad does it hurt—and will you love and live again?

A breakup envelops one in a feeling of abandonment and desertion. Is anyone listening? Surely God hears your plaintive cry for help. God heard the cries of the writer of Psalm 22:1–

5, My God, my God, why have you forsaken me? Far from my deliverance are the words of my groaning. O my God, I cry by day, but You do not answer; And by night, but I have no rest. Although the Psalmist was not bemoaning the loss of a relationship, we feel the intensity of that cry for help.

A more modern interpretation is

Thursday: drowning in love
Friday: drowning in doubt
Saturday: drowning
Sunday: God, I can't drag myself to church this morning.
Please make a house call.[1]

We are all familiar with the beginning of a relationship. The initial jitters, the infatuation, the puppy love. But how do we know when it is done? There are no guides, lessons, or teachers that prepare our hearts and minds for endings. The death of love is not talked about as readily as the beginning. Why ever dream of a day when love says goodbye?

The pain of abrupt endings produces thoughts that range from sorrow to suicide. Some folk walk around in a funk for weeks, others want to jump off a bridge. There has to be a godly, sane way to handle the words "I don't love you anymore."

∞ Case 1 ∞

Kevin, a tall man with anger in his eye, was the first at the microphone. "All I want to know is why," he said pointedly at me. "If God loves me so much, why did God allow this to happen?" Kevin was engaged to the woman of his dreams.

Intensive premarital counseling had taken place. A major wedding had been planned, and an even more major engagement ring rested on the left hand of his wonderful woman. Then, with no warning, Kevin's fiancée phoned him and said she didn't love him anymore and could not marry him. Kevin's voice was cracking when he added, "We kept this relationship biblically grounded. What is God punishing me for?"

Kevin's teeth were clenched and his eyes were bulging. He wanted to explode, and I knew he needed the opportunity to vent the anger and get it out of his system. A hurting man has few positive outlet options for his pain.

"I've lost money, manhood and morale," he continued. "The wedding ceremony costs are nonrefundable, and I was paying for everything. The three-carat diamond engagement ring, which I want back, is also nonrefundable. I look like a complete fool in front of everyone. My family and friends are laughing at me. They told me she was no good for me, but I would not listen. They never liked her in the first place. I need to get over her and find someone new."

∽ Diagnosis ∾

I told Kevin that the first step toward a solution was seeking help: "I applaud your bravery. You could have carried the pain of this breakup around inside you, and it would have eaten you alive. The pain of aloneness and the rejection that you experienced understandably overcomes you now. You need to unload some of it in order to recover."

Kevin was grieving which can be unfamiliar territory for a man. "So just how is a man supposed to grieve? To grieve is to feel, and men are not supposed to feel, they cope."[2] Grieving is a process—a normal and necessary process for recovery from loss. There is a beginning, a middle time, and an ending to your grief. This process goes on to greater or lesser degrees for weeks, months, and sometimes years.[3]

There are 10 stages of grief according to Elisabeth Kübler-Ross. There are the *early stages* that include shock, disbelief, denial, anger, hidden feelings, and negotiating for change. The *middle stage* includes a turning point of facing the truth and understanding. The *later stages* include acceptance, forgiveness, and making a plan. The *final stage* is recovery—and that is all about taking the action.[4]

Kevin's ex-fiancée took him for a ride. She was true to her own feelings about no longer being in love with him, but she squashed his heart flat in the process. I said, "Kevin you are also experiencing shock. This means you were caught unaware. You lost your emotional balance. As a result you may feel a bit uncertain, or unsure of yourself for a while. That is normal too.

"You may forget your keys, misplace your wallet, drop a glass or misspell your own name—several times in a row. Absentmindedness, forgetfulness, and clumsiness are frequently experienced after a loss.[5] Rejection is another bitter pill that you must swallow. Rejection inflicts a deep ache in the self-esteem. It makes us second-guess ourselves, and ask what we did wrong. Rejection lowers our ability to think well of ourselves and flattens our inner joy. It makes us ask, How can I even love myself, if someone else couldn't?"

∽ **Prescription** ∾

If you have been dumped, the only way that you will be able to face tomorrow and put one foot in front of the other is by

giving all your pain to God. Our God specializes in helping
hurting people. When you decide that it is too heavy a burden
to carry, God will lift it from your shoulders and remove it from
your spirit as well. Take your mind off the hurtful incidents and
fill it with the positive possibilities of God. In Philippians 4:8
we read: *whatever is true, whatever is honorable, whatever is
right, whatever is pure, whatever is lovely, whatever is of good
repute, if there is any excellence and if anything worthy of
praise, dwell on these things.*

The one act that will cure all that ails you is one of life's
most difficult—forgiveness. "Whenever you can, as soon as you
can, forgive the other person. You do this not for the other
person, you do this for yourself—your peace of mind, and the
quality of your future relationships."[6]

Kevin needs to forgive her for hurting him, and then forgive
himself for the strident feelings that he harbored in his heart.
In 1 Peter 3:9 we read, *not returning evil for evil, or insult for
insult, but giving a blessing instead; for you were called for the
very purpose that you might inherit a blessing.*

∽ **Case 2** ∾

The phrase *I don't love you anymore* is not just used between
lovers; it also has a painful sting when it is uttered among family
members. Although blood is thicker than water, ending love
hurts.

Brittany was the next person to come forward to speak. A
tender 16-year-old girl, we erroneously assumed that her problems of love were centered on some boy that she was crazy over.
We were wrong. She had been told "I don't love you anymore"
by the most important person in her young life—her mother.

Brittany's world came to a standstill when her mom forced her to move out of the house. Her mom's boyfriend wanted to move in and there was not enough room for the both of them. The loss of a parent by death is incredibly difficult for young people. When the loss is deliberate, the ending is a nightmare. Brittany was distraught, hopeless, and helpless.

"My mom and I never were that close in the first place. She was always fussing and cussing at me," Brittany explained. "But when she told me to pack my stuff and get out, I knew for sure that there was not a bit of love in that ice heart of hers. She loves that jerk. He made her choose between us. Any mother who picks her man over her own flesh and blood is low."

Brittany, 16, and her momma, Jody, had had a rocky relationship from the beginning. Jody gave birth to Brittany behind bars during her last stint in prison. Nobody taught her how to parent, so she did the best she could. She had hoped to straighten up, live the clean life, and be a regular citizen. She successfully held down a job cleaning high-rises downtown and avoided her former drug addict friends, until she met Ray. From then on, things went downhill.

"Ever since my momma started hooking up with this guy, my life has been hell. Things at home got bad. She stopped spending time with me, I had to get to school the best way I could. She started giving all her money to him, so our lights got cut off a couple of times, too. She would go out with him and come home days later. But when he got put out of his place, he moved in with us and life got real bad. He gets high all the time. And is a nasty, nasty man.

"One night he got up out of momma's bed and came into my bedroom. I felt someone standing over me, woke up, saw him and I screamed my head off. Momma came running into my room and he told her that I asked him to be with me. She believed him and went ballistic. The next thing I knew my stuff was packed and I was on a bus, going to live with Granny. Granny brought me here tonight. She thinks I need the help because I stopped going to school, stopped talking on the phone to my friends, and I sleep all the time."

∞ Diagnosis ∞

Brittany is a victim of her mother's mistakes. What is happening is not her fault. Although her mother was trying to do the best she could, it was not enough. Jody sounds like she is wrestling with her own challenges. I explained to Brittany, "The situation in your household has created a lot of sadness inside you. It has depressed you. And you have a right to be. The trauma that you've experienced is more than enough to drain any of us of joy and life.

"I suggest that you may be depressed because of the behavior changes that you told us about," I told her. "Pulling in and away from other people is one of the symptoms. While mild depression seems common for most teenagers, it can signal severe problems. Depressed adolescents often don't go out, stop talking to their friends and family, and become inactive, drop out of peer relationships, spend a lot of time alone in their rooms.[7]

"Brittany you are not alone in your feelings, several researchers estimate that upwards of 10 percent of children and adolescents have at least one depressive episode.[8] Even more interesting is that, even though you and your mom are at odds, you may have something in common—depression."

Many children who are brought for counseling or who experience problems in school have a parent who is depressed. Indeed, children of a depressed parent are more likely to develop a depression themselves. Conversely, treating a parent's depression helps to resolves children's depression in many cases.[9]

∞ Prescription ∞

"The road to restoration for you, Brittany, starts with you embracing this truth," I said. "You were treated like a piece of trash, but you are priceless. The Bible tells us that we are fearfully and wonderfully made. You did nothing wrong, yet life dealt you an unfair hand. Your depression can be remedied with counseling. A trained counselor can help you sort through your feelings and empower you to look at your situation in a positive way. We believe that the Lord moves in mysterious ways. The move to your grandmother's house may be the blessing in disguise that God has planned for you. The relationship that you have with your grandmother is pivotal for you. She seems to be someone who cares for you and is willing to do what it takes to get your life back on track.

"I also suggest that you and your mom consider joint counseling. She is challenged right now with decisions and consequences. She will come to herself in the future and realize the mistakes she made when she put you out. When she reaches out to you, ask her to go to counseling with you. That way the two of you can come up together. She loves you, she just can't figure out how to express it. She needs help too. Your family unit can be put back together again. The stressing events in your lives can be reduced. Hold on to your hope."

We closed this session of the Love Clinic thankful that we serve a God who never stops loving us. In 1 John 4:7 we read, *Beloved, let us love one another, for love is from God; and everyone's love is born of God and knows God.*

Let us pray
Dear God,
Even though we are not treated the ways we would like here on Earth, just knowing that Your love never fails gives us joy. Come inside our sorrow and fill up our empty places with Your nonstop concern for us.
Amen

Chapter 10

❧

SAY WHAT?

"You don't hear me!" the preacher roared to the congregation. They, in delightful response, shouted back, "Yeah. Yeah!" The preacher's rhetoric told the gospel truth about us and our relationships. We don't hear! Something has prevented us from hearing, listening, and valuing what others are saying to us. That's why in part rates of divorce, teen pregnancy and domestic violence are high. Communication is the key for progressive, positive relationships. If we can't talk to each other, we can't do anything at all.

When women ask for love, men think women want sex. When men ask for their space, women think they are being abandoned. Women want to talk, men feel like women are smothering them. Men say they will call later, women think "later" means later on that day when it may mean later that month. She raises her voice—he stops talking and walks away. She overreacts—he underperforms. We have a mess on our hands. We've got a psychological self-hate that makes us hate the opposite sex and ourselves. Disagree? Just listen to talk on the street. Women are verbally disrespected by men. Men are denounced by women. There is no love in our conversation. There is no love between us. We need an incentive to talk to each other the right way.

Some say many problems are generational because many parents did not speak to each other correctly. Momma and Daddy cussed, fussed, and walked around the house mad all the time. Some of us have painful mental images of our parent's hostile, combative discussions. Dr. George Edmond Smith wrote candidly about the inability to communicate in his book *More Than Just Sex*. He too suggests that our dilemma is historical. He could not recall his mother and father ever "talking calmly, joking or discussing issues in a civilized manner."[1] He wrote, "they often argued loudly, gesturing and pointing accusingly, making my heart race with fear."[2] Dr. Smith deduced that his own poor communication skills with women stemmed from what he saw and learned as a boy. This awareness enabled him to make changes.

The Bible offers us plenty of helpful guidelines in the area of communication, if we'd only hear what God is saying to us. Our tongues are powerful, never take them for granted: *So also the tongue is a small part of the body, and yet it boasts of great things. See how great a forest is set aflame by such a small fire* (James 3:5)! Give each person a chance to speak, don't cut them off, assuming you know what they will say: *He who gives an answer before he hears, It is folly and shame to him* (Proverbs

18:13). Speak kindly to each other. The way we say something has a lot to do with our problems: *A gentle answer turns away wrath, but a harsh word stirs up anger* (Proverbs 15:1).

God made men and women differently, but in that difference we can find delight. Men and women may communicate differently, but we have to keep trying, and not give up.

∞ Case 1 ∞

Tara and Kelvin's ability to communicate was reduced to nothing. After three rocky years of marriage she was an animated yeller. He was a consistent shut-it-down man. No one had ever told them that there was a better way. They had never seen a better way. Their style of arguing threatened to end their marriage. Now, arguing in and of itself is not bad. Healthy couples argue. Arguing can be a means of sharing differing points of view. The difference is in the way or style a couple argues. Do they go for the other's jugular or do they seek resolution? Do they throw things at each other, or do they sit down calmly and lay their points before each other?

Tara and Kelvin have what's called a "harsh startup." Their initial comments to each other are coarse, and things go downhill from there. How we begin our conversations sets the tone for the whole dialogue. Statistics tell us that "96 percent of the time you can predict the outcome of a conversation based on the first three minutes of a fifteen-minute interaction. A harsh startup simply dooms you to failure."[3]

"When we get home from work that's when things start to go bad," Kelvin said. "We can't even have a simple conversation about our day anymore. Anything sets her off. She gets to talking wild, and pointing in my face. I go watch television, so I won't have to hurt her. I hate to go home," he said.

Kelvin grew up in a home with a similarly mild-mannered father and a hot-tempered mother. He knew the drill. Daddy would sit in the den, relaxing from a hard day teaching school, and Momma would come in from her job at the post office snapping and popping about something. Like clockwork, his mother would verbally attack his father. Kelvin's stomach would knot up.

"I tried to get Tara to go and talk with our pastor about this, but she is too embarrassed. She thinks that if the pastor knew we weren't getting along at home he would ask us to step down from our leadership positions. I say she's wrong on that matter too," he added.

Tara stood beside her husband boiling like a hot kettle. With every word Kelvin spoke, her agitation increased. Finally, she exploded. "Why can't you ever remember what I say to you?" Tara demanded to know. "You can be so ignorant sometimes. I didn't say that about our pastor. You think you know everything, but you don't. You hear me talking to you, don't you?" she said rolling her eyes, working her neck, and pointing her finger in his face. By this time Kelvin had blocked her out entirely.

Tara grew up hard and her style of arguing was meant to defend her not only verbally, but also physically. Growing up she watched her mother stand up to the often violent men in her life. Her mom had to be loud and strong if she wanted to survive. Her mom had to be aggressive and insistent if she wanted things to happen. Tara learned that being in a relationship meant telling men what to do and what not to do. Otherwise, things did not get done.

∞ Diagnosis ∞

Tara and Kelvin were two well-meaning, pleasant people, but they were uninformed. They lacked a basic framework to communicate. They demonstrate that a couple needs classes and instruction to develop and maintain successful relationships. They also demonstrate the truth of Proverbs 25:24: *It is better to live in a corner of the roof than in a house shared with a contentious woman.*

I listened carefully to the fireworks of their conversation/yelling match. It had four characteristics that marital therapists tell us doom it from the start: criticism, contempt, defensiveness, and stonewalling.[4] These four negative elements guaranteed that the two would hurt and harm each other with words and behavior.

I told them, "You are so deep into the negative interaction that you don't realize it. It has become very common to you, and you assume that every couple behaves like this. They don't.

"Tara, you are the classic ballistic woman. You are always on the verge of going off on your man about something. You are always just waiting for him to make a wrong move. You are ready to pounce quickly. You grew up distrusting and disgusted with brothers. The ones in your neighborhood were about nothing. Always trying to get over or get some, and you, naturally built up a wall of defense to protect yourself. You were wise to protect yourself, but Kelvin is your man. He deserves the softer side of you," I explained. "Your complaining is really criticism."

Complaining addresses specific actions of your spouse, the criticism escalates to include character assassination.[5]

"Then," I said, "you moved on to eyeball rolling, neck working, and finger pointing. Surely you know this does not help the situation. These actions convey disgust. It is virtually impossible to resolve a problem when your partner is getting the message you're disgusted with him.[6] As a result of the drama you just served up to Kelvin, he has tuned you out and off. His body language told us all that he was not engaged in the conversation. His eyes were down, his head was turned away. He is doing what is known as stonewalling. It's acting like he couldn't care less about what you're saying, if even he hears it.[7]

"Kelvin, you are repeating your childhood, because your father was a quiet man who was married to a loud, argumentative woman," I explained. "Although your dad did not stand up for himself, you should. This does not mean using physical force or giving Tara some of that drama back in her face. I want to see you engage in the dialogue in a helpful way. Your absence sends her the message that you just don't care, but I believe that you do. The yelling takes you back down memory lane to the knots in your stomach as a kid, you love this woman, but her out-of-control yelling is too much."

∽ Prescription ∾

For Tara and Kelvin, I suggested a step-by-step method of talking to each other that teaches how to communicate and not to condemn. This sounds elementary, and it is. But it's what you need to get the basics of conversation.

This simple exercise is called the "Stress-Reducing Conversation. Spend 20–30 minutes a day after work talking to each other and sharing personal concerns about your job or other issues. Do not discuss the marriage or what you don't like or what somebody did.

Take turns. She talks for a while, and then you talk for a while. Don't give unsolicited advice. Stay on the topic and don't analyze. Show genuine interest. Give eye contact and use a pleasant voice. Communicate understanding. Sound supportive. Take your spouses' side. Let them know that you are a team. Express a "we against others" attitude. Verbalize that you are with them. Express affection. Hold hands, hug, and kiss. Validate emotions. Assure them that their feelings are OK.[8]

I admonished them both, "Tara and Kelvin, you are a beautiful couple. Don't let the war of words, and the eruption of emotions mess up your marriage. You have the brains and the strength to work it out." They thanked me and took their seats.

∞ Case 2 ∞

Another couple came forward with a less dramatic, but equally painful communication issue. Shauna did not feel loved. Her husband, Trent, a shoe-store manager and part-time carpet layer, was puzzled by her ongoing complaint. Their six-year marriage was one that kept him on edge. "I have provided for her," Trent said. "She said after the kids were born she wanted to be a stay-at-home mom. I took another job so she could do that. She said we needed a larger house. I found another house with more room. We live in a comfortable house and we both drive nice cars. And she does not feel the love. Somebody help me please!

"To make matters worse," Trent added, "when I finally get home, from my two jobs, there is no hug, no kiss, no nothing!"

Shauna came to the microphone to speak, juggling two small children as she talked. "It might not make sense to anyone here but me, but even though Trent has done a lot for me, I still don't feel like he loves me," she said as tears ran down her cheeks. "We are members of a Bible church that teaches wives to stay at home and husbands to work and support. We were finally able to do that and I appreciate the extra job Trent got to help out. But still something is missing. And with God as my witness, I need to find out what it is," she declared.

∽ **Diagnosis** ∾

This couple is firmly engaged in the work of sustaining a marriage, but neither of them feels loved or appreciated. We know that "the need to feel loved is a primary human emotional need. For love, we will climb mountains, cross seas, traverse desert sands, and endure untold hardships."[9]

Shauna and Trent are a prime example of the fact that all male-female communication is not verbal. Some of the most potent acts are nonverbal. We must be "willing to learn your partners' primary love language if we are to be effective communicators of love."[10] There are five primary love languages: words of affirmation, quality time, receiving gifts, acts of service, and physical touch.[11]

Love languages speak directly to the need of your spouse, without all the guesswork. Lots of couples go through an entire marriage with each spouse trying to guess and figure out what the other spouse wants from them—when, all the while, the matter could be addressed by learning the love language. Love is the essential key to everyone. The communication mistakes we make stem from our need for love and the way that love gets mangled by our humanness.

∞ Prescription ∞

"I hate to say it, but the house, the cars, and the stay-at-home status are still not enough," I said. "Although material possessions sound appealing, if we do not possess the emotional soothing, we will be wanting. Trent, Shauna is wanting, wishing, and waiting for approval from you or a compliment here or there. Her love language is words of affirmation. She needs encouraging words from you that affirm her as she is. There is power in your words. You have no idea what they mean to her. She is not asking you to suck up. She needs to hear you tell her when you come home what a great cook she is, and how nice the house looks. That is love to her," I said.

To Shauna I said, "Just as you have been hurting from a perceived lack of love, Trent is also hurting. He has gone above and beyond to give you what you want in this marriage. He works two jobs! But I am hearing him say that the clean house, hot meals, and well-kept children are not enough. He needs you as well. It sounds like his love language is physical touch. For some individuals, physical touch is their primary love language. Without it, they feel unloved.

"With it, their emotional tank is filled and they feel secure in the love of their spouses.[12] Meet him at the door with kisses and hugs. Let this good man know that you are for him and not against him."

We concluded this Love Clinic with scriptures from 1 Corinthians 13:11. *When I was a child, I used to speak like a child, think like a child, reason like a child; when I became a man, I did away with childish things.*

Let us pray

Dear God,

Sometimes we don't understand what our partners are saying and sometimes they don't understand us. Please Lord, stand in the middle and help us to straighten it out. Stand all around us and be that translator who enables us to hear and understand and love as we should.

Amen

Chapter 11

CAUGHT IN THE ACT

During the time it takes to read this sentence, somebody else's man and somebody else's woman are pairing up to cheat at church. Exchanged winks across a crowded sanctuary signal the next rendezvous. Notes written on offering envelopes speak when lips cannot. Emergency board meetings that last into the wee hours of the night forge illegal alliances.

Adultery is alive and well in the church. One Christian survey indicated that 65 percent of men and 55 percent of women will have an extramarital affair by the time they are forty.[1] Lord knows what awaits us after age 40. Infidelity creates pain that engulfs more than just the two cheating participants. It can rip families apart and even split a church. I know discussing adultery in an open forum is critical. Experts who have studied infidelity tell us that there are basically three types of affairs.

There are the Class One affairs, the one-night stand. There are the Class Two affairs, the love relationship that starts off as a friendship and grows because of a deficit in the marriage. And there are the Class Three affairs, which involve sexual addictions.[2]

Sometimes the sin is so habitual it becomes a generational sin, and is passed down like a set of silverware. Check your family tree. You may discover an uncle who had an upstanding position in the church, but maintained another family on the other side of town, or an auntie who was the pastor's secret wife. In the Bible one of the first believers to fall into adultery's trap was King David. According to 2 Samuel 11, one gorgeous spring evening King David strolled across his penthouse terrace and noticed a beautiful maiden bathing. He lusted for the woman, inquired who she was and whose she was. She is Bathsheba, he was told, wife of Uriah, who was away at battle. David was aroused, and summoned her to him. The two had sex, and Bathsheba conceived a child. David plotted Uriah's death, and Bathsheba became his wife. There is nothing new under the sun.

There is a sick attraction to the secrecy and forbidden nature of adultery. Proverbs 9:17 agrees, by telling us that *Stolen water is sweet; And bread eaten in secret is pleasant*. The consequences are high. "An affair is a sign of need for help—an attempt to compensate for deficiencies in the relationship."[3] Cheaters give numerous reasons why they've done the dirty deed. This list is endless, so I'll just share a few: emotional immaturity, self-doubt, destructive pride, unresolved conflict, and unmet needs. Cheating seems to have become a national pastime for clergy and laity, male and female.

∾ Case 1 ∾

Is it possible to have an affair, and keep your clothes on? Yes. These are called emotional affairs. Charlise was one of the first to come forward to share, and that was her testimony. This attractive 30-year-old probation officer had a husband at home and a husband at the job, too. She admitted that she had just gotten out of something that had her running like a chicken with it's head cut off. "I did not know if I was coming or going," she said. "But God brought me out of it, and I have got to help somebody else.

"Now somebody is probably asking, what if two people are just spending time talking at work? That sounds innocent doesn't it?" she asked. "Well think again. One of my male co-workers was going through some problems at home. He knows that I teach a Bible study and that I am in the Word. He saw me carry around my Bible during lunch break, so he knew that I knew Jesus. So when he first asked me for advice, I was happy to give it. It's an honor to represent Jesus on the job. I was confident that whatever his problem was, Jesus had an answer. But I'll be honest, the more he shared his personal details, the more I shared my personal details. Over time I began to look forward to our conversations. I'd go to work early and stay late to squeeze in as much time with him as possible. I put my husband and kids on the back burner so I could sit and think about that man. Oh, my mind was blown."

Charlise is known around her church for her energy and zest. She chairs the youth department and can be found counseling troubled girls at all hours of the day and night. Charlise grew up in a home filled with inconsistencies. Her parents were very religious, but their home was barren of love. Her mother rarely had kind words for her, and they had a cold, distant relationship. Unfortunately, her father did not keep his distance and sexually molested Charlise for many years. All of this took place under the guise of a stable, Christian home. Charlise married to get away from her frigid and frightening family. She went with the first man who asked her. Even though her husband was a good provider, and loved her dearly, his love could not soothe Charlise's agonizing past.

"Things blew up when my husband found a note from the guy at work in my car. I was too scared to lie anymore. So I told the truth. But since we didn't do anything I didn't see what the big deal was. But I saw later on, when my husband cried. I realized how much he loved me and how much my stupid actions hurt him. It was not worth it," she said.

⸙ Diagnosis ⸙

"Charlise, it's a blessing that you did not take that affair any further," I told her. "The Lord was truly with you." By looking at Charlise's background, we can see how it impacted her behavior. All of our actions are related. Things from the past don't stay in the past, they creep into the present and make themselves known again. Survivors of incest wrestle with a number of issues that they may not be aware of. Survivors often repress or push the pain away from their conscious mind to their unconscious mind, where it is less likely to bother them. Survivors "often experience depression, a constant sense of being on guard, and difficulties with trust and intimacy."[4]

Persons in these so-called platonic affairs rob their marriages of emotional energy. They will save their topics of conversation to talk over with their other friend, rather than their spouse.[5] They also struggle with feelings of betrayal when they have sex with their spouses. But these are the hardest affairs to recover from because there is no guilt.[6]

Charlise's age and gender group has the fastest growing rate of infidelity—young, married women. "Many of them have been molested or are the adult of children of divorce. They are looking for marriage to make up a deficient that comes from their childhood."[7]

Author William July II has done extensive research on emotional infidelity. He concludes that women are more likely to emotionally cheat than men: "For many women, keeping sex out of the affair can give a sense of control, as if they haven't completely lost their heads. That's especially true if the man wants the sex and the woman refuses."[8]

⬭ Prescription ⬭

I said, "While we do not use incest as an excuse, we can understand what led you astray. To get a household back in order after an emotional affair consider the following steps. They are challenging."

1. Tell your spouse about the affair.

2. Separate from the other person. This may mean changing your job or church.

3. Write a letter to the other person ending the relationship. Let your spouse see it and sign it.

4. Make a commitment to the betrayed spouse to never see or telephone the other person again.

5. Cease all communications with the other person by e-mail, phone, fax, pager, or cell phone.

6. Allow your spouse to monitor all forms of communication.

7. You and your spouse should give each other 24-hour schedules of daily activities.

8. Discuss finances jointly so that money cannot be spent on the other man/woman without being detected.

9. Spend leisure time together.[9]

∽ Case 2 ∾

Temptation is the cornerstone of infidelity. Without it, we'd all live in the land of solid marriages. Even though we pray that God will lead us not into temptation, most of us know the way anyhow. It's been said that temptation is our lifelong companion. For Remington, temptation was a way of life. Even though he was the business administrator of a mega-church, his walk did not match his talk. This 39-year-old, flamboyant accountant could easily balance the church books, but he could not balance out his temptations with the power of Jesus Christ.

"We all agree that sex starts in the mind. Right? Well, my thoughts quickly grew into act, after act, after act," he said. "I have run my wife out of town with my cheating. She tried to stay, but it was too much."

The power, the glamour, and the money of the pulpit splashed over on him, and he sopped up every drop. Remington is the only child of a prominent Episcopal leader in the Midwest. He traveled frequently with his father to church events, and carefully watched the way the men in authority handled the women who flocked to see them. They were treated callously and carelessly, yet the women seemed to enjoy it and returned for more. Remington listened to how the men spoke disrespectfully about women. These church leaders were his classroom on women and relationships.

"I was wrong. I was so wrong," he said. "I mistreated God and my wife. How could she have put up with me for so long? I humiliated her in front of the congregation so many times with my fooling around. She'd pray for me. I'd hear her calling on the Lord on my behalf. Maybe her prayers can save me. But why should they? I was so far gone with all the other women that sometimes I'd be in bed beside my wife wishing that she would just die in her sleep so I wouldn't have to deal with her and I'd be free to see the others. The others? They were women from the church who were using me to get to the Bishop. One woman thought that by sleeping with me, she'd be sleeping with the Bishop next. I was so caught up in that mess that I agreed with her."

∽ Diagnosis ∽

I told him, "Remington, you are a serial adulterer. You just can't help yourself. Infidelity is in your blood, and it has got to come out. The years you spent with your father and the other church leaders warped your understanding about women. Rather than treasuring women as you should, it sounds like you hold us in contempt. Only a strong sense of loathing could drive you to treat so many women so poorly. Your wife bore the brunt of your irresponsibility. Your actions stripped her of pride down to the core. One can only imagine how she is feeling. We need to have prayer session expressly for her."

As a man in power of a church, Remington was privy to access that few others gain. Power and money make men do things none of us would ordinarily do. Men have an unwritten code of acceptance for cheating. Stepping out, or tipping around, or cheating in the next room has never been quite as wrong if men did it. After all, he is a man, many say. He can't help himself, others declare. This type of attitude has allowed many an adulterer to behave badly. The large church atmosphere also contributes. People get caught up in the crowds of thousands, the television broadcasts, and such. These are not negative things, but they can have a negative effect on people.

∞ Prescription ∞

"Even though we are tempted all the time, we must learn to handle it," I said. "Temptation is always of Satan, never of God. Just ask Adam and Eve in the Garden of Eden or Jesus about his experience in the wilderness."

You can't stop the devil from singing his bewitching songs in your ear, but you don't have to join him and sing a duet . . . You can't stop the devil from dropping his brats on your doorstep and knocking incessantly on your door. But you don't have to open the door, take them in, warm them, clothe them and feed them.[10]

Men like Remington need a complete reorientation on women. He would benefit from a revised understanding of who, what, and why women exist. Women were not put on Earth to be used and abused. We were put here to be loved and to be cherished.

If a woman is perceived as subordinate and not entitled to a man's respect, there is less chance that there will be open communication and honest love within a relationship. If men continue to see the woman as a femme fatale, then they prevent themselves from developing a true loving partnership. Fear replaces feelings of love as a form of protection from being betrayed.[11]

There is hope for couples in these situations. Prayers that a spouse sends up to heaven regarding the marriage are not in vain. But before a man can reunite with his wife, he needs to seek the Lord and ask for a cleansing of his mind, spirit, and soul. Remember the words of Jesus in Matthew 26:41: *Keep watching and praying that you may not enter into temptation; the spirit is willing, but the flesh is weak.*

We concluded this session on a high note by focusing on the power of God as found in 1 Corinthians 10:13: *No temptation has overtaken you but such as is common to man; and God is faithful, who will not allow you to be tempted beyond what you are able, but with the temptation will provide the way of escape also, so that you may be able to endure it.*

Let us pray
    Dear God,
    Blot out our sins and forgive us of our wrongdoing. Help us to honor You through our marriages. Give us what we need to be supportive spouses who never give up on love, and who believe that we can do all things through Your power.
    Amen

Chapter 12

YOU CAUGHT YOUR SPOUSE IN THE ACT

You caught your spouse with both hands in the cookie jar called adultery. Maybe she was in the arms of another. Maybe you came home from work early and found him in your now defiled bed. Maybe you spotted her car at what was your favorite restaurant. Maybe he confessed his cheating ways to you when he could not hold the truth in any longer. Maybe you found a discarded love letter, or overheard a phone message. Perhaps it was an e-mail or a receipt for a gift that did not come to you. Maybe it was a trip to the doctor's office that detected a sexually transmitted disease. Possibly it was the woman on the phone yelling about being pregnant. No matter how you discover your spouse's infidelity, you need to determine how you are going to react.

The Good News is that most marriages survive infidelity.[1] It's just a matter of *how* they survive it. Does the couple claw each other to death, or calmly and prayerfully work it out? I've seen couples that bounce back from affairs like nothing ever happened. Then there are others that are still huffing and puffing over an affair from thirty years ago. Not only do couples react differently, one sociologist noted that men and women react differently to the news that their spouse is cheating. "Men are likely to be self-righteous and angry, less likely to see the affair as an act against them, tend to take action. Women are likely to be hurt; they absorb the news and wonder what's wrong with them."[2]

Who can forget that biblical scene in John 8 where the woman is caught in adultery? The scribes and the Pharisees bring her to Jesus, urging that she meet the traditional fate of being stoned to death. Jesus responded by stooping down to the ground and writing in the sand. They begged him for an answer. Jesus stood and said, *He who is without sin among you, let him be the first to throw a stone at her* (John 8:7). One by one the men left. Jesus told the woman, *I do not condemn you either. Go. From now on sin no more* (John 8:11).

We know the public side of the story, but what happened when she got home? Wow. Can you imagine those fireworks? There are the classic reactions to adultery such as *freezing*, where we refuse to see what is going on and live in denial, or *frying*, where we burn inside with self-pity and self-righteousness. Sometimes we are *folding* or leaning on the cheating spouse for more support. Lastly, there is *fighting* or retaliating, taking revenge and blaming.[3]

Anyone who has caught his or her spouse cheating is wounded, fragile, and weary. They need to be treated with care, concern, and Christian love and respect.

∞ Case 1 ∞

Mack discovered that his wife of eight years, Kendra, was having an Internet affair. He noticed that she decreased the amount of time they spent as a family because she was always on the computer. "At first I did not notice it at all. Lots of people were excited about the Internet," he recalled. "They were all surfing around and discovering new sites and what-not," said the mild-mannered banker. "We used to sit and visit new sites together, just to get a laugh or learn something. I thought we had a good thing going. We'd send e-mails to our kids in college and relatives. It was great. But all of a sudden Kendra would slip off to use the computer and she did not want to talk about the sites she was looking at. When I tried to press her, she started cursing me, and told me never to touch the computer again. Kendra has never, never acted like that before."

This is the second marriage for Mack, 44, and Kendra, 40. They both have college-aged kids and have worked hard to blend their families. They met at a church singles retreat and dated two years before marrying. They wanted to make sure that it was real love.

"She's been acting real strange. She up and quit going to church. She said she was not getting anything out of it anymore. This is the same woman who bought every audio and videotape that comes out of our church. She'd play them so often that they would wear out. So one day, while she was out, I went to some of the sites she was visiting and I got the shock of my life. There were porn sites. She was into some sick stuff, and apparently she had gone to enough chat rooms to pick up like-minded men. They had become Internet lovers. I was thrown for a loop. I love her, but I am clueless about this."

∽ Diagnosis ∾

I told him, "Mack, it sounds like your wife Kendra may be what is known as a cybersex freak or a cyber addict." These are people who throw their lives away so that they can spend time on the Internet. Cyber addicts give themselves completely to the Internet. The Internet becomes their world, and all else means nothing to them. Much of the allure of the Internet is its anonymity. People are free to be whoever they want to be and go wherever they can click to without any repercussions. Because it is not real, their conscience doesn't kick in to warn them of danger. The unending variety of information on the Internet intrigues people, but the problem arises when the variety takes them in over their head. The secrecy, the taboo topics, and the freedom from conscience are a dangerous combination. This behavior can become addictive, because it unlocks our sinister side.

Without question Kendra's sinister side was unlocked and unleashed. An active churchwoman who plays the pastor's taped sermons until the sound is gone is an active churchwoman who is into the Word. A woman like that would not abruptly stop going to church unless something untoward is going on.

The betrayed partner will experience a range of emotions including shock, disbelief, rage, hurt, devastation, disillusionment, and intense sadness.[4] An affair like this is not only a blow to pride, but also a shock to the system.

∞ Prescription ∞

For a marriage facing this challenge, the cybersex surfing must stop. Therapy is the best step for overcoming such an addiction. In addition to therapy, there are several steps to take.

1. Talk with your spouse and find out why it happened. It may be helpful for you to know this. Knowing may lessen your pain and help move you forward. You need to know why, so you can begin looking at yourself and your marriage candidly. Perhaps your wife needed to be affirmed, maybe she was seeking sexual fulfillment, and maybe she didn't feel attractive. While none of these reasons are justification, they can help explain her actions.

2. Listen carefully to your spouse's reasons. While they are not right, you can have a role in providing what she is missing in your marriage. "Married people seek out or succumb to affairs when they feel devalued and less than fully alive. They are bored. Overburdened. It amounts to being very lonely, and it can happen in a household full of kids and a babbling spouse in which there is a backbreaking schedule of fun things to do. People who have affairs have the child's longing to be touched, caressed, held, hugged and kissed, whether they can admit it or not."[5]

3. Forgive. Encourage your spouse to forgive herself. Forgiveness does not let anyone off the hook, or look the other way, or say the actions were OK. Forgiveness allows you both to move on with life. Marriages cannot thrive without forgiveness. "People who stay together but don't

forgive live in shallow, meaningless relationships."[6] The Bible tells us, *Whenever you stand praying, forgive, if you have anything against anyone, so that your Father who is in heaven will also forgive you your transgressions* (Mark 11: 25).

∽ Case 2 ∽

Marcia, 25, also caught her spouse in the act. Her annual visit to the gynecologist informed her that she had contracted a sexually transmitted disease. The doctor's prescription cured the infection, but it would take more than that to cure her broken heart. Her life as an NBA player's wife was challenging to say the least. The rewards—a luxurious house, exciting travel, expensive clothes, and life in the limelight—far outweighed the problems.

"When my doctor told me that I had syphilis I nearly fell off of the examining table. Do you know how embarrassing that is? The doctor took one look at my face and did not say anything else. I snatched my cell out and called DeAnthony right on the spot—legs in stirrups and all. I let him have it with both barrels. All he could say was 'It wasn't me!' This confirms what I suspected for a while. He is messing around on me."

This college beauty queen met her husband during her senior year at the university. He was a freshman, straight off the farms of Alabama. Even though a lucrative professional basketball contract hung over his head, Marcia fell in love with the man and not his money. Dubbed the prettiest woman on campus, Marcia was also highly sought after. The two had what appeared to be a storybook romance. DeAnthony was a humble and somewhat naïve guy in those days. Oh what a difference six figures can make.

"I've got a very religious mother," Marcia continued. "She is in church almost every day, and I know that I am at the top of her list. My becoming the wife of a professional athlete means a good life for me and for my family. We had to struggle when I was a kid. Sometimes we did not know where our next meal was coming from. Things are different now, and I don't plan for them to change. I knew that there were lots of women chasing after him, but he said that he'd settle down with me. I am prepared to ride it out. Hell or high water, this man is mine. The problem is he won't stop seeing her, and she won't stop calling our house."

⚮ Diagnosis ⚮

"Marcia, it appears that you are married to an immature man," I said. "His emotional and psychological development have not caught up with his physical development. He looks full grown on the outside, but on the inside he is a confused, bewildered little boy. Some sociologists suggest that many men are under-developed and retain adolescent characteristics because of over-protective mothers or even overindulgent mothers.

"Your marriage is young and there are tremendous pressures on the both of you to look good and present a flawless image. These demands take a toll on you both and force you to seek unrealistic goals for yourselves."

✂ **Prescription** ✂

"DeAnthony sounds like a young man with potential, who will benefit from the strong boundaries and guidelines of a Christian marriage," I told her. "The two of you need to take your eyes off of the fast life and put them on the everlasting life from Jesus Christ. Your marriage needs the stability and predictability that a church membership offers. Join somebody's church and dedicate your lives and your marriage to Christ."

In a situation like this, the first order of business is holding on to your sanity. Keep a positive attitude. Pray for strength during this ordeal. Prayer changes things. As the Lord is working on your marriage, don't become a doormat. Don't let your husband see you as weak and pathetic. Hold your head high. From the author of *The Divorce Remedy*, I share some great suggestions:

1. Stop chasing, pushing, pleading, and pursuing your spouse. This makes the other person more attractive.

2. Stop talking about the affair. The more you ask, the more pressure he may feel.

3. Do your best to be perky, and in good spirits when he is around. The other woman is quite happy when he is around.

4. Keep busy. Do things you enjoy. Spend time with friends. Have fun.[7]

Eventually your spouse might realize that the grass is *not* greener on the other side.

We closed this Love Clinic with the words from 1 Peter 3:9: *Not returning evil for evil or insult for insult, but giving a blessing instead; for you were called for the very purpose that you might inherit a blessing.*

Let us pray

Dear God,

Our hearts are heavy and the ones we love shatter our confidence, but we know that Your love for us is supreme. Bind up our wounds and piece us back together again. If it is Your will, repair our marriage and renew the love that we once shared. It is only by Your power that renewal is possible.

Amen

Chapter 13

YOUR MARRIAGE FAILED, NOT GOD

Your marriage has come to a screeching halt. It crashed into hardship and split clean in two. It's over. What do you do now? Where do you go? How will you go on? You are able to do and go, because God is still with you. Your marriage failed, not God. I have said these very words to divorced adults over the years. It's my job to shake them out of the paralysis that sets in after the love is gone. To hear some folk tell it, the divorce is the worst thing that can happen to a Christian. They see it as a no-win solution to a deteriorating marriage and prayers that seem to go unanswered. As a result, divorcees experience shame and spiritual confusion. They feel victimized by their faith, betrayed by their God, and penalized because they chose to end their marriages.

In and of itself, divorce is not a good thing. It is not a God thing. God hates divorce, because it breaks the vows of marriage. It is God's desire that husbands and wives unite in holy matrimony till death parts them. God wants marriages to last forever. God wants the love between the spouses to remain strong and vibrant all the days of their lives. Unfortunately, life does not always lead us in God's path. Unexpected twists and turns take us in unwanted directions and to undesired destinations. It hurts to be pulled away from God's plan. That's why divorce is painful.

Conservative interpretations of the scriptures say that divorce is not an option, period. You remain married no matter what. Anyone who dares to break with this viewpoint is labeled faithless and is asked to leave the church or even put out of the pulpit. That's why divorced people are treated like lepers at some churches across the nation. Can't you see the gossipers now? "If that man had prayed more, he could have held on to that woman." Or "if they had been tithers, they would not have gotten a divorce." Or "she's not a real Christian, she got a divorce." The teachings of Jesus in Matthew 5:31 are the center of the controversy. Here, Jesus talks about divorce in no uncertain terms. In a conversation with a group of religious leaders who already had a long running feud on the topic, Jesus said, *everyone who divorces his wife, except for the reason of unchastity, makes her commit adultery; and whoever marries a divorced woman commits adultery.*

At the Love Clinic, we believe that Jesus affirms the sanctity and power of marriage, but that Jesus knows something about human failure, too. That's why we offer divorcees healing, hope, and help. They've had enough hell in their lives. Divorce is alarmingly high. At the Love Clinic, we see our mission not only to help people to love, but to help them to heal.

∞ Case 1 ∞

Monty, a handsome, articulate television journalist, is going places. That's why Tiana seemed like the perfect wife. She was on the fast track toward being named metro editor at the local paper. The two were great together. They understood and appreciated the fast-paced, unpredictable news business and loved the adrenaline rush that accompanied a breaking story. Sadly, their opulent wedding, covered by all media outlets in town, plus *Jet* magazine, unraveled nine months later.

"I feel cheated," Monty said, twisting his features grimly. "Tiana lied to me. I was duped, I was had. She was not what she said she was. She was a lesbian. Why did she keep that to herself? She had no love interest in me at all. Why play with my emotions?" he asked tersely. His eyes squinted and his lips barely moved, he was so enraged.

The divorce was devastating. The same media that told the world about the wedding also broadcast the divorce news along with all the sordid details. The adoring public quickly turned ugly. Monty's news broadcast took an unexpected dip in the ratings. He was humiliated. He had trouble focusing on the teleprompter as he read the news. His mind frequently wondered away from on-air interviews. At chance meetings, the former couple are very adversarial. "If I could hurt her, I would," he admitted. "Maybe that will bring up the ratings." Monty knew that something was seriously wrong. "I went to my pastor for his advice. He told me that I should have come to him sooner and that divorce was a big mistake. He said that I could have changed Tiana's ways with faith, but I have let God down. My marriage is over, I look like a fool, and my pastor has dissed me. What am I supposed to do now?"

∽ Diagnosis ∾

"Monty," I said, "there is so much going wrong in your life right now that it is tempting to tell the Lord to just forget it. In the midst of what is bad can be a blessing," I said. "Don't blame yourself," I continued. "You were used as a cover-man to help your ex-wife's image in the city. She used you like a stepping-stone. Yes, you were played. What are you going to do about it?"

Anger is a common emotion, and, while justified in Monty's situation, it's important not to linger in it too long. Anger has a way of dissolving self-esteem and robbing us of our courage. Anger will not help him get over his divorce and move on with his life. Anger, often accompanied by thoughts of revenge, is a dangerous place to dwell. It is a convenient place for divorcees to rest instead of moving on in their healing process. It is easy to rest here, because you can toss blame, you can call your ex names, and you can tear down your ex's character from this vantage point. Unfortunately, what is also happening is that the anger is seeping inside your soul.

∽ Prescription ∾

I told Monty, "If you do not heal properly from this tragedy, your soul will be warped and crooked. You will be unable to receive real love when it does come to you. Someday the right woman will come along. I want you to be ready for her and not running from her because of your wounds."

Here are a few tips I gave him to help move on with life:

- Let go of the past. Most people experiencing divorce feel that they are just not going to make it. They feel this way because they spend most of their mental energies racing backward into the past or forward into the future.

- Don't get trapped in your child state. "It is easy to get trapped into childish behavior with a former spouse. Childish behavior with a former may involve temper tantrums, getting even, telling lies, jealousy, fighting, etc. These things can happen when we forget who we are."[1]

- Be a thermostat and not a thermometer. You can affect change in this situation. You have the power to control your atmosphere. You've probably heard this all your life. Now it's time to put the words into practice in a challenging situation.

The circumstances of Monty's divorce were low-down and dirty, but he doesn't have to be. Remember the words of Romans 12:2: *And do not be conformed to this world, but be transformed by the renewing of your mind.*

∞ Case 2 ∞

Anger is a concern for many singles like Monty. For other singles, like Tracey, accepting the fact that she was no longer married is harder. Still wearing her wedding band, Tracey came forward to tell her story. The 45-year-old woman once had it all. "I enjoyed the good life while I was married. I thought we had a great marriage. We had a profitable business together. We were together twenty years. We didn't have children, so we were free to travel, and we dined, and we shopped all the time. My world was rocked when Craig came home one day and said, 'It's over.' It can't be over. I am not ready for it to be over. Who said he could end it like that?" she asked mournfully.

Craig had fallen out of love long ago and had already mentally and emotionally abandoned the marriage. Tracy was left to play catch-up to him.

"Craig took my pride when he left. More importantly, he took the business, too. I was so in love that I didn't bother to read the contract. My name is nowhere to be found," she added. Not only was she divorcing, but also she was rapidly descending the economic ladder. She traded in a four-bedroom villa in an exclusive gated community for a one-bedroom apartment in a modest section of town.

"I believe that there is no failure in God, and when I told the prayer warriors at my church what Craig had done, they told me to hold on to my marriage. They told me to ignore the divorce papers, pray, and fast and things would turn around. What happened to my prayers?"

∽ Diagnosis ∽

"Tracey, the major issue for you is accepting the fact that you are a single woman. Wearing the ring won't bring him or that fine house back. In fact, the ring serves as a bitter reminder of the way it used to be. You can't go back. I am hearing despondency, despair and self-disgust in your story. You are feeling about as low as one can go. Maybe the words of the Psalmist describe where you are."

O Lord, the God of my salvation, I have cried out by day and in the night before you. Let my prayer come before You; Incline Your ear to my cry! For my soul has had enough troubles, and my life has drawn near to Sheol. I am reckoned among those who go down to the pit; I have become like a man without strength, Forsaken among the dead. (Psalm 88: 1–5).

"We know that the Lord heard the cries of the Psalmist—and God hears you, too."

⤜ Prescription ⤛

"The best way to handle a divorce is to seek newness, rather than staying the same old person," I suggested. "The end of a marriage creates a person that you may not like. In the name of Jesus, become someone better. In Jesus, we have the power to rise up from failure and falling. In 2 Corinthians 5:17 we read, *Therefore if anyone is in Christ, he is a new creature; the old things passed away; behold, new things have come.*

"Visit new places so you can see new sights. Looking at the same places, people, and things may keep you feeling the same. Make new friends by perhaps joining a new organization. Join a new church. If you release what has been, the future may open up for you.

"Also, don't let other people superimpose an identity upon you. It's sometimes easier to become what other people want us to be rather than what we really want to be. Form your own identity. You are you—not what someone else is or thinks you are."[2]

We ended this session by focusing on God's healing power.

In Psalm 147:3, we read, *He heals the brokenhearted And binds up their wounds*. We knew that somehow, someway, God would heal that crowd of hurting people.

Let us pray

Dear God,

Divorce has forced itself into our worlds. It is an uninvited guest that causes sorrow, tears, and confusion. We need You, Dear Lord, to be our comforter and our strength. Though others may not understand or approve, we know that if You are with us, we can make it. Dry our tears, and be the lifter of our heads.

Amen

Chapter 14

⟡

KEEP IT HOT

Is there sex after marriage? As the joke goes, What's the best food to curb your sexual appetite? Wedding cake.[1] While sex is not the only reason for marriage, without it married couples can act like enemies rather than soul mates. Sour and dour expressions tell the world what it must be like to live in that house. Where is the love? Where is the spark of affection that kept this couple's hands on each other constantly?

Some of the freeze comes from the church. God invented sex, but church folk act like it's from the devil. Rarely do pastors talk candidly about marital sex, and as a result congregations have suffered. The religious community has demonized sex and made it wrong, ugly, and nasty. In actuality, it is a form of worshipping God. It's even been said that our climaxes are praises to God in the temples of our bodies! Who else could have crafted a penis and a vagina to function with such precision and accuracy and create such passion?

We Christians have become so heavenly bound that we are no earthly good, and we are missing a good thing. Experts say that marital sex is better sex.[2] This is because "married people have more incentive to invest time and energy in pleasing their partners, have more time in which to learn how to please them, and are more confident that the gifts they give to their partners will be reciprocated."[3]

The emotional commitment of marital sex is also worth noting. "Emotional commitment improves one's sex life in other ways as well. For example, sex with someone you love literally doubles your sexual pleasure: You get satisfaction not only from your sexual response but from your partner's as well."[4]

According to the *National Sex Survey*, "married people have both more and better sex than singles do. They not only have sex more often, but they enjoy it more, both physically and emotionally, than do their unmarried counterparts."[5] The survey found that "43 percent of married men reported that they had sex at least twice a week. Of the surveyed wives 39 percent of them had sex two or three times per week. These numbers exceed the sexual activity of single adults."[6]

∞ **Case 1** ∞

Ruth and Mark sleep in separate bedrooms, and have done so for the last two years of their ten-year marriage. These 46-year-olds own a computer programming firm, and are the picture of life and vitality at church and in the civic groups they participate in. But their sex life is nonexistent. Their daughter, Kim, was abducted and murdered five years ago, and their lives have not been the same since.

"Since Kim was taken from us, I have lost my life too. It seems like I can't even get up in the morning," said Ruth. "Mark does not seem to be hurting at all. He has moved on with his life, and I cannot. I think about Kim all the time and nothing else. Who can even think about sex at a time like this? We should be mourning our daughter, not swinging from the ceiling in ecstasy. What's wrong with him?"

Mark said, "In the past we had a great sex life, but now it's almost like we can't stand to be near each other. The sex used to give us such joy. Now when I try to touch her she goes berserk. She kept up the hysteria and so I encouraged her to leave our bedroom until she gets herself together."

⤜ Diagnosis ⤛

Ruth is what is known as a *celibate wife*. She has decided to live without sex due to a negative situation in her life. Either husband or wife can impose celibacy on the marriage. It can be created by any number of incidents, such as infidelity, boredom, loss of respect, alcoholism, illness, spiritual growth, verbal abuse, or incompatible sex drives.[7] Experts call the condition inhibited sexual desire (ISD), "a psychological term for an often-complex problem manifested as the loss or lack of interest in sex as a result of some stressful life situation."[8]

Traumatic events can impair a couples' sexual relationship. The death of Ruth and Mark's daughter has stolen Ruth's joy. It pains her to think about happiness because of her child's death. Joyful feelings also inspire guilt.

Pleasure, especially sexual pleasure, is easily relegated to the back burner when hearts and minds are burdened with feelings brought about by events such as death of a loved one, financial insecurity, family difficulties, loss of a job, or medical problems . . . [Stressful events] can so consume your thoughts that the sensual images needed to stimulate sexual desires have been literally wiped out of your mind . . . [9]

Mark's situation is different. Typically, men are interested in sex regardless of what is going on in their lives. They can contract the mumps, have a broken leg, lose their job, and not have eaten in a week, but their sex drive does not diminish. The male sex drive is so strong that a relationship without sex seems meaningless.[10]

∽ Prescription ∾

I told them, "You have a strong foundation, and there is something we can build on. Your sexual relationship has a chance at revival because of four key factors: the ISD is stress related, your marriage is stable, there is good will between you, and you are able to communicate.[11]

"Ruth, I'd recommend stress relief therapy to assist you in handling the feelings of loss from your daughters' death. A professional counselor can lead you into a place of acceptance. The death of your daughter should not be the death of your marriage. You both have your lives ahead of you, and really need each other for support, now more than ever. Ruth, maybe you are taking out your frustration on Mark for Kim's death. This behavior is destructive and will take you nowhere.

"Mark, it is vital that Ruth view your ongoing sex drive as

an innate part of manhood rather than callousness and indifference toward the family tragedy. It is vital that you invite her back into the bedroom. Just as sex is a man's number one need, affection is the woman's top requirement.

"For most women, affection symbolizes security, protection, comfort, and approval, vitally important commodities in their eyes.[12] Talk to her, assure her of your love. Hug her, hold her hands. She is still deeply grieving and should not be alone."

Time apart sexually can do a marriage no good. Even Saint Paul, considered by some to have a low view of sex, explicitly advised Christian married couples that they should not abstain from sex for long periods. He emphasizes the reciprocal physical union marriage represents in 1 Corinthians 7:4–5. *The wife does not have authority over her own body, but the husband does; and likewise also the husband does not have authority over his own body, but the wife does. Stop depriving one another, except by agreement for a time, so that you may devote yourselves to prayer, and come together again so that Satan will not tempt you because of your lack of self-control.*

◌⟡ Case 2 ⟡◌

Greg and Rochelle had exasperated expressions on their faces when the topic of keeping it hot was raised. At first I thought I had insulted them somehow. Marital sex is to be celebrated, right? With this couple, sex is nothing but a hassle. He is frustrated. She is angry. For the past six months this couple's lovemaking has been a series of refusals and arguments. Greg has transformed from the affectionate, loving husband of five years, into an arguing, accusing spouse. Rochelle is hostile, shrill, and almost ready to pack her bags and leave.

"What do you do when your man changes on you? He is not the man I married," declared Rochelle, a 36-year-old petite real estate broker. "The man that I married was full of passion and always had time for me. Now he volunteers for extra hours at work, and gets home after I am asleep. And he'll try to slip into the bed without even saying anything to me. I am so puzzled by him. He was hot before. Now he is ice cold. Have I done anything? Greg always talked to me, and we were partners in every aspect of our relationship. Now it's like I don't even know him."

Greg, a tall, muscular, high school football coach was experiencing sexual dysfunction and was petrified with fear. Always a star athlete and a ladies' man, Greg felt like his world had ended. "How was I to tell my beautiful, sexy wife that I could not perform anymore?" Greg asked. "We had a strong sexual relationship. She may have tried to divorce me. I was scared out of my mind. I panicked every time I turned into the driveway of the house. I had to avoid her. If she got too close to me, I'd start a fight so she'd leave. My strategy worked for a while, but I'm tired of running from her. I love her. I just don't know what else to do."

⤳ Diagnosis ⤳

Greg's sexual dysfunction cooled off the sexual aspect of his marriage because of its impact on his self-esteem:

> The psychological impact of being unable to achieve an erection can be devastating; especially if he is uninformed about the nature of his condition . . . he is confronted with a "failure" that

can emotionally parallel death. Impotence can deeply wound a man's psyche.[13]

Most problematic was the fact that even though Greg had seen a doctor and found out that his problem (impotence) could be relieved by medication, he was reluctant to take the medicine because it might not work. He has been shut down by fear.

I explained to him, "Greg, you have shut out your wife, the prescribed medication, and the power of God. Those are three things that you need desperately. Your fears have been allowed to become giants. A portion of your fear was needless. Your wife is not going to leave you. She loves you, but needs you to open up and talk to her."

Impotence affects 30 million men in the United States. It affects some men to a greater degree than men of other ethnic groups because of the prevalence of cardiovascular disease and diabetes, conditions capable of causing impotence or sexual dysfunction.[14] Black men "tend to be affected most severely, or those who define themselves in sexual terms, and overcompensate in negative ways."[15]

∞ Prescription ∞

"Your self-esteem cannot be defined by your sexual performance," I told Greg. "Look at other areas of your life for success. Remember that you are a child of God, and there is no failure in God. Your fears have taken over your entire life and they've reduced you to a little boy.

"A husband is more than just a sex machine. Your wife loves you and is standing by you. Joining forces with her to get through this battle will be essential. In fact, your wife is the cornerstone of support. She is the pillar of strength in your home. Go and visit the doctor and take her along to hear what the doctor tells you. Don't give up on having an active sex life. Once you have obtained a physical diagnosis and gotten help the two of you may be back together sooner than later. The key is never give up and never stop talking to each other.

"Be fearless, and think on the words of another couple found in the Bible in the Song of Solomon or Song of Songs. There we find beautiful and erotic love poetry. Why don't you and your wife try this on each other when you get home?"

For Greg, I recommended Song of Solomon 7:1–2,5:

How beautiful are your feet in sandals, O prince's daughter! The curves of your hips are like jewels, The work of the hands of an artist. Your navel is like a round goblet, Which never lacks mixed wine; Your belly is like a heap of wheat fenced about with lilies. Your head crowns you like Carmel, and the flowing locks of your head are like purple threads.

For Rochelle, I recommended Song of Solomon 5:10–12, 14:

My beloved is dazzling and ruddy, Outstanding among ten thousand. His head is like gold, pure gold; His locks are like clusters of dates and black as a raven. His eyes are like doves beside streams of water, bathed in milk . . . His hands are rods of gold Set with beryl; his abdomen is carved ivory inlaid with sapphires.

We ended this Love Clinic with more words from the Song of Solomon 7:8–9, which celebrates hot, sizzling marital love: *And the fragrance of your breath like apples, and your*

mouth like the best wine! It goes down smoothly for my be-
loved, Flowing gently through the lips of those who fall asleep.

Let us pray,
    Dear Lord,
    We are grateful for the gift of marital sex and we ask that
    You bring us into its full enjoyment. Guide us as we struggle
    with problems and issues that block our physical relation-
    ships. Ultimately give us solutions so that we can maintain
    the marital flame.
    Amen

Chapter 15

I Still Do

Remember this question? *Will you have (this person) to be your wedded wife/husband? To have and to hold, from this day for-ward, for better, for worse, in sickness and in health, to love and to cherish?*[1] Your answer was *I do.* And if you remain in 0love with that person, if asked the question above again, will you answer, *I still do?*

Marriage vows are uttered before God and a host of family, friends, and others because we have found the person of our dreams and we want to spend the rest of our lives together. Hold on to your love. Whatever state it is in you can work it out. No matter how many years it has been or what issues you are dealing with, you can make it. Repeat after me: *I still do.*

Here's reason to continue saying "I still do," realize that your great marriage explains that gleam in your eye and that pep in your step. Studies tell us that married people have lower rates of mortality than the non-married; they also feel healthier than singles, too. That same study revealed that married people are simply happier than singles as well.[2]

It's a myth that you can fall out of love with your spouse. What really happens is that the love dwindles. It is no longer a priority in your life. But don't forget: "Love is a living thing. If you nurture it, it grows. If you neglect it, it dies. The number one cause for the breakdown in marriages in our country is that people don't spend enough time together."[3] Review your weekly schedule. Do choir practices, usher meetings, soccer games, golfing, tennis, or hiking take up more time than attention given to your spouse? If so, slow down and rearrange your daily agenda in favor of the marriage. This will loudly and lovingly proclaim "I still do."

Unfortunately, Christian marriages don't get the support that they deserve. Folk who are able to remain married deserve a standing ovation. No one talks about it, but marriage is hard work. The erroneous word on the streets is that all you have to do to be married is find somebody good looking, and the rest is easy. Marriage is an uphill struggle on both spouses' parts but it is the most rewarding struggle of your life. Taking the time to be constantly loving, caring, supportive and to communicate with your spouse is more than a notion. We are always at war with the flesh that seeks our own selfish reward. But through the power of Jesus Christ we are able.

Many married couples don't want to air their dirty laundry in public. There is a pervasive stigma that says only people with problems attend marriage seminars. The element of shame covers us, and we will go out of our way to avoid any appearance of problems. To soften the offensive image of counseling, I liken marriage to an expensive automobile like a Mercedes or a Rolls-Royce. I ask reluctant couples, "If you owned a Mercedes or a Rolls-Royce would you take care of it?" They say sure. I continue, "A car like that needs to be taken to the dealership for routine check-ups. Would you take it in?" They say sure. I say, "Your marriage is a Mercedes. Your relationship is a Rolls-Royce. Do you take care of it? Do you take it in for routine check-ups?" There is no response. We must shake off the shame, and embrace the reality that problems don't go away. The only way to fix them is to face them. If you love your spouse, and there are issues, going to counseling tells your spouse "I still do."

The couples following were happy and had no plans for divorce—they just wanted to talk it out and hear other perspectives.

∞ Case 1 ∞

Nina and Eddie raised a testy topic among married folk: money. Married folk have concerns when the change is strange. There are common issues, like who spent all the money at the mall, or why didn't you bring your paycheck home, or who authorized you to give cousin JoJo the money for bail bond? But Nina and Eddie's topic blew us away. They wanted to know what to do when the wife makes more money than the husband.

"This is an issue in our home," Nina said. "There is friction about it, but we have never come to any conclusion. I love him and he loves me. But my paycheck is dividing us, slowly but surely." This 34-year-old legal eagle was flying high in the land of lawyers. Armed with her Harvard law degree, she had ascended up the ranks to her current post. Nina's family is proud of her, her friends are proud of her, but her husband does not quite know what to do about it. Nina is from a middle-class family. They were not rich, but they lived a comfortable life. In her understanding money is to be made, saved, and spent on the family.

Eddie, 36, makes an average attorney income at a small firm. He is committed to offering low-income persons access to decent legal services. Eddie grew up poor in the Deep South. His mother cleaned houses and his dad worked when he could. Eddie watched his father's embarrassment when his mother's meager income had to carry the family. That pain took up residence in his mind and never left, which is why his wife's status rubs him the wrong way.

"My wife is a superstar. She has a big title, a big office, and an even bigger salary. I am proud of her, but sometimes I feel like her glory puts me in the cold, cold shadows," Eddie explained. "I don't like the shadows at all. And her paycheck keeps me in that shadow. I do alright as a lawyer, but when I look at her, I don't feel alright."

Nina added, "One solution that we've considered is me stepping down from the position of counselor general. I can find another job. This way there will be peace in my home. We both want to start a family one day. Maybe this is God's way of telling me to stop working."

∽ Diagnosis ∾

Eddie is intimidated by his wife's money, and feels small beside her perceived success. The two share the same profession, so a degree of competition is inevitable. What does money mean? Does it symbolize status, power, love, life? We all have deep-

seated memories of money, and sometimes we project those feelings onto our spouses.

A successful woman can be a threat.

> Brothers without a lot of confidence, without an internal
> strength that doesn't wither depending on which way the winds
> blow, will have their egos crushed by a successful, striving sistah
> who appears to be on top of the world. They will constantly feel
> an incessant need to compare themselves to her, to see how they
> measure up. And of course they will forever come up far short.[4]

In our society, men who are with women who make more
money get picked on. People talk about Oprah Winfrey's man,
Stedman Graham, like a dog. They speculate on how she is
underwriting the budget of his very existence. People like to
crack on Susan Taylor's man Kephra Burns, too. He is frequently seen in *Essence* at Taylor's side with a grin on his face.
Both of these men are role models for brothers with self-
confidence. Any man who can hold his own beside a powerful,
high-profile woman is an awesome brother.

∞ Prescription ∞

"Eddie, the bottom line is that you shouldn't even begin to care
what others think about your wife's salary," I told him. "If that
is the root of the problem, let's kill that root now. There is a
needless penalty placed on the high-income earning woman by
the man. She's been blessed. She is soaring and she needs her
man right beside her, helping and encouraging her to do even
more. To harp on the income issue too long may wear down
her self-esteem. Think of all the pressure she faces on that high-

paying job. She does not deserve to have to come home to criticism for doing well.

"Another positive of her earning more is that you know she is not with you just for your money. Lots of men are worried about gold diggers and users. This sister loves you, not your wallet. You need confidence in who you are, regardless of the wallet. Nina's quitting her job will not accomplish anything."

To Nina, I said, "To keep the peace in your home, keep on working but always work to keep your man feeling important. That means that you will never hold over his head the fact that you've got more zeroes on your paycheck than his. You will never talk down to him or attempt to put him down as you stand on your salary. The money is a blessing. Put it in a joint account and enjoy it."

And to both of them, I said, "Overall, your marriage is not in any trouble. The financial disparity in your incomes is a small road bump that we have effectively reduced. You two can tell each other 'I still do' by continuing to work and work on the marriage."

Studies tell us that marriage and work are a profitable combination. Marriage makes husbands and wives more successful, say the studies. "The wage premium married men receive is one of the most well-documented phenomena in social science. Husbands earn at least 10 percent more than single men do and perhaps as high as 40 percent more. The longer men stay married, the fatter their paychecks get."[5]

∞ **Case 2** ∞

An older couple raised an issue that arises over time as Christian couples study and grow in the Word, but at different levels and speeds. Alicia and Travis were both active members of their church. Their three children were grown and out of the house, and the empty-nesters threw themselves into church participation. Travis's involvement was more of the physical—parking lot ministry, usher board, and youth chaperone. Alicia spent most of her time there in the Word. She'd hungrily completed every level of Bible study the church offered. She was hungry for the Word. It built her up.

When they married twenty-five years ago, she was a young girl of 19 and Travis was the older man she had prayed for. At 40, he was the father figure she'd longed for. Alicia's dad died when she was a baby, and she felt an emptiness for male support and love. Travis was a guiding force, a teacher, a mentor, and more for her. He instructed her in the ways of marriage based on Ephesians 5:22, in which women are to be submissive to their husbands. His word was the law in their house, no questions asked. Alicia gladly followed his directions—he was the undisputed head of their house. The hierarchical style of marriage was effective for twenty-five years. They reared their children and had peace. Yet as Alicia grew in her knowledge of scripture, another view of marriage emerged from the scripture—a marriage of equality. She noted that Ephesians 5:21 urges couples to submit to each other. She wondered why was that passage overlooked in favor of 5:22?

"What do you do when you're tired of being the submissive wife?" she asked. "Spiritually I am chafing under this rigid marriage," Alicia explained. "What seemed comfortable back then is beginning to irritate me now. I wanted to know, why couldn't I make any money decisions? Why did I do all the diaper changing, dishwashing, cooking, and cleaning over the years alone? After sitting there looking dumb for twenty-five years, I finally

wised up. The God that I serve gave me a brain and I am supposed to use it and my spouse is supposed to let me use it. But
he won't."

Travis did not have too much to say. The silver-haired, dis-
tinguished gentleman was having his world rocked by a wife
who has gone from submissive to shouting. "She's changed. She
didn't act like this before. I wonder where the real Alicia is.
This is crazy," he said. "The man is the head of the house. That
goes without question. I don't know what Bible she is reading
from, but women should know their place," he said.

∽ Diagnosis ∽

I've seen Christian husbands and wives struggle for the headship
in marriage instead of pursing collaboration. They claw and
scrape their way into being the leader, when all the while Christ
is the true leader. Just as women are looking for the exit signs
away from traditional marriage, men are looking for ways to
shift or share the responsibility.[6]

Alicia is bold and Travis is frightened. The traditional and
generational roles of their marriage are being reversed. She is
no longer the little girl that Travis married and raised. She has
matured and seen a new side of life. Alicia has grown up and
become her own woman. Her husband provided well for her,
and with his support she blossomed and thrived. His support
enabled her to take all the Bible classes at church. The information that she has learned is testing their marriage.

◌ Prescription ◌

"All marriages need to become flexible to accommodate growth. Your love is certainly strong enough. In order to achieve an authentic intimacy as husband and wife you will benefit from the collaboration or peer marriage. Here you submit to each other, you seek to please the other, and one is not constantly checking the other to see if they are still running things. You can do this. Mature adults have no business investing time trying to be in charge. Be in love."

Look at the scriptures regarding marriage with the conviction that Jesus, who ultimately defined the role of women, defines marriage.[7] This style of marriage will empower both spouses to embrace change, growth, and say to the other "I still do."

We concluded this Love Clinic with the words from Philippians 1:9, *And this I pray, that your love may abound still more and more in real knowledge and all discernment.*

Let us pray
　Dear God,
　We love our spouses and we love You. Show us new and creative ways to demonstrate our love. Give us the energy and desire to please our mates, and let our actions be pleasing in Your sight.
　Amen

Chapter 16

SINGLE PARENT BLUES

Between a rock and a hard place is where many single parents permanently reside. With one hand grabbing the shreds of their self-esteem, the other clutching the kids, they are barely holding on. Overwhelmed by the sheer responsibility of the emotions from the divorce, child rearing, and working, some single moms and dads are singing the blues. Their song is not a faint one. Single parent homes are America's norm now, with more than 16 million children living with one parent.[1]

Hagar of the Old Testament book of Genesis (chapter 16 and 21) is the first single parent that I know about. She had it bad. Abraham, her baby's daddy, turned on her and put her and the baby Ishmael out of the house with nothing to live on except a loaf of bread and a jug of water. When things got desperate and her son's cries for help went up to the Lord, the Bible tells us that God stepped in, rescued the duo, and showered them with Good News of a bright future if they could hold on to their faith. The key is to hold on to our faith, even when all else looks bleak. How does a parent not only help himself or herself through such a difficult time, but also help a child? Take a tip from Hagar—do what you have to do to survive, hold on to your children, stay in touch with the Lord, and press on regardless.

The children of divorce also are often the casualties of the relationship war. The impact of Mom and Dad splitting up can either make them cry or breathe a sigh of relief, but it will impact their future. If possible, we want to prevent them from repeating their parents' divorcing history.

Findings from the survey of 8,590 adults were presented at the American Sociological Association meeting recently in Toronto. The survey showed that among adults whose parents had two or more divorces, 67 percent divorced themselves, and 26 percent had two or more divorces. Among adults whose parents divorced and remarried once, 58 percent divorced themselves, and 19 percent divorced at least twice. Among adults raised in intact homes, 41 percent divorced, and 9 percent divorced two or more times.[2]

∽ **Case 1** ∾

Daemon's seven-year marriage crumbled into divorce, and he got custody of the children—which was no surprise to him or anyone who knew the troubled couple. His ex-wife, Suzette, was pretty and intelligent, but she also was a crackhead. She was high as a kite at their wedding, and never really came down.

She was always out with her girls, searching for the next high. There was no way the courts would give her the kids. Suzette didn't even show up for the custody hearing. She already knew what would happen. Her drug-induced absences around the house told the rest of the family that she had other priorities. Daemon, 28, was striving to do right in a society that did not offer him much support.

"I had a feeling that Suzette's drug thing would be trouble down the road," he said. "But she said it was just on the weekends, and that it was no big deal. She was just hustling me. I put up with all of the stealing and lying I could take. She had to go. I divorced her. It's my boys and me now."

Daemon and the boys are active members of a church that sponsors a single parents gathering every week. "Thank God for the church. They have been a lifesaver for me. There are a couple of other guys in the group, and we have really bonded. They split with their wives and they have custody of their kids, too."

Although he has a support group, there are still issues that must be addressed, like dealing with the pain his boys feel. "It hurt like hell when I had to tell those boys that Mom was not going to be there. They still don't understand. My six-year-old keeps an angry expression on his face. He is fighting at school, and he keeps asking me, what did I do, what did I do, Daddy? My four-year-old is clingy. He holds on to me constantly," he explained.

∞ **Diagnosis** ∞

"Daemon," I told him, "you deserve a standing ovation! At a time in America when many fathers are running from parental responsibilities, you break that negative trend, by standing tall and proud," I said. "Even though you are doing the right thing, you are clearly overwhelmed with your emotions and caring for the boys. Each of your boys is affected differently by the divorce according to his age group. Your youngest is clinging to you excessively because he realizes that something is wrong and he does not know what it is. Preschoolers don't have the reasoning power to understand the emotional turmoil he feels.[3]

"Your older son has the angry look because he is probably livid about the divorce, but realizes that there is nothing he can do about it. As a result he will probably strike out at other children. Or the quality of his schoolwork may suffer. You may see a host of other negative effects like angry or violent outbursts especially at dinnertime and bedtime, times when the family is together.

"Or they began to have bouts of bed-wetting, hyperactivity and withdrawal.[4] Begin and maintain an ongoing dialogue with your sons' teachers about their behavior and helpful ways to assist them."

∞ Prescription ∞

In the aftermath of divorce, children need their parents in a variety of ways, particularly as a spiritual guide. The emotions that swirl within them can be tamed by a stable, loving, Christian environment. Professional counseling is always an option. I'd recommend rebuilding the family unit around the Word. They need something to hold on to. Let them hold on to your hand and God's unchanging hand.

"Be the faithful father who is there for them," I told Daemon. "A faithful father will teach them how to pray. Take them by the hands every day and pray for them and with them. A faithful father will be their role model. Always take the high road regarding their mother. Let them see her for themselves. A faithful father will show them that faith makes a difference. As you lean on God for your own inner healing, they will emulate you."

As Deuteronomy 6:6–7 tells us, *These words, which I am commanding you today, shall be on your heart. You shall teach them diligently to your sons and shall talk of them when you sit in your house and when you walk by the way and when you lie down and when you rise up.*

As much as men and women suffer in a divorce, children need special consideration. Following are guidelines for respecting your child's rights and needs.

Divorced Children's Bill of Rights

I have the Right to know that I am unconditionally loved.

The Right to know that I didn't cause my parents' divorce.

The Right to know what caused the divorce.

The Right to the security of knowing where I will live and who I will live with.

The Right to be aware of how stress affects my life and how I can adapt to it in a healthy way.

The Right to be a kid and not be afraid of being myself.

The Right to have the guarantee that my physical and emotional needs will be met.

The Right not to be a victim of the past marriage and not to be used as a pawn between my parents.

The Right to have my own space for privacy to ensure respect of my person.

The Right to have a normal household routine and discipline to warrant a sense of security.

The Right to possess positive images of my parents so that I
  can love each parent equally.
The Right to have access and time with each parent equally.[5]

∞ Case 2 ∞

Single parenting was not agreeing with Brandy. This high-strung
33-year-old schoolteacher and mother of 10-year-old twins, was
about to snap. "I have to get to work, pick them up from
school, take them to soccer practice, attend church events, plus
find time for my sorority meeting, nails, hair and massages. It's
just not working," she said tersely.

Brandy's marriage to Bradley was ended by his affair with
his secretary. The divorce felt like somebody had pulled the rug
out from under her feet. Their divorce was not a private incident—it was played out before the membership of a sizable
church because her husband was the pastor and she was the
first lady. Members took sides and some left the congregation.
As soon as the divorce papers were signed, Bradley married his
mistress and moved to serve as pastor at a much larger church
in another state. He had a new wife and a new life. Brandy had
the kids, was still in the community that had witnessed the dis-
solution of her marriage, and had no time for herself.

She finds herself short-tempered with the twins. Tense and
frustrated she began to experience hair and weight loss. "How
was I supposed to be a single mother?" she asked. "I cannot
carry this load by myself. It was tough enough with Bradley
here, but now that he's gone, what am I supposed to do? I have
to be mother and father. My folks say it will be all right, but I
don't see it like that."

∞ Diagnosis ∞

"Brandy, you have been through the fire—but you did not get burned," I counseled, "give God some praise. I encourage you to keep your head up as a former first lady, despite what you've been through. God knows your struggles and God has not brought you this far to leave you. As a single mother, you are trying to do it all, but you can't. It's tough to admit, but when we try to take on too much, we wind up having nothing. Single parenting can overwhelm any of us, and we feel underprepared to handle it. Your short temper is a signal that you are taking on too much. Your twins need you to be calm and in charge for them."

∞ Prescription ∞

Single parents need to find balance in their lives that will address their needs as well as those of the children. Remember these important points:

1. Don't attempt to be a super parent.

2. Find a support group in your area for you and for the kids.

3. Present a balanced view of marriage to the kids.

4. Don't disrespect the children's father or men in general.

5. Take a break from your kids occasionally. They need the space and so do you.

6. If you choose to date do so from a position of strength and not weakness. Meet your dates at neutral sites away from the children for at least six months. Make sure the ones that they meet are going to be around for a while.

We ended this Love Clinic focusing in on the reality that children are a gift from God and singing a new song. We read Psalm 33: 1–3: *Sing for joy in the Lord, O you righteous ones; Praise is becoming to the upright. Give thanks to the Lord with the lyre; Sing praises to Him with a harp of ten strings. Sing to Him a new song.*

Let us pray
Dear God,
We are parenting alone, but You are always with us. Help us to be caring, loving, and responsible providers who can look out for our children, but also for ourselves. Give us the courage to keep walking, sometimes where there is no light.
Amen

Chapter 17

SAINT BY DAY, FREAK BY NIGHT

Can a scripture-quoting, Bible-carrying, God-fearing person also be a freak? Yes. Can a lewd, lustful, and ludicrous person also be a saint? Yes. There are men and women who sit piously and respectably in church on Sunday morning, but at night, or out of sight, they engage in ungodly acts. The pastor may preach a sermon about deliverance from temptation, but as soon as church is over he may give himself unto temptation.

Almost everyone has a positive side and a negative side. Two opposing attitudes cannot peacefully dwell inside one person. Chaos will ensue. This struggle is nothing new. Believers in Christ have wrestled for centuries with the need to do the right thing, even though the wrong thing feels good. In Romans 7, Paul writes vividly of his struggle with inner natures that duel for attention:

But I am of flesh, sold into bondage to sin. For what I am doing, I do not understand; for I am not practicing what I would like to do, but I am doing the very thing I hate. But if I do the very thing I do not want to do, I agree with the Law, confessing that the Law is good. So now, no longer am I the one doing it, but sin which dwells in me (Romans 7:14–17).

For I joyfully concur with the law of God in the inner man, but I see a different law in the members of my body, waging war against the law of my mind and making me a prisoner of the law of sin which is in my members. Wretched man that I am! Who will set me free from the body of this death? Thanks be to God through Jesus Christ our Lord! So then, on the one hand I myself with my mind am serving the law of God, but on the other, with my flesh the law of sin (Romans 7:22–25).

A freak is someone who engages in what we consider bizarre, unhealthy, immoral, or illegal sexual acts. Freaks range from those who make obscene phone calls, to those who are hooked on prostitutes. The freaks come out at night, say the rappers, but at other times their acts are simply perpetrated out of sight of other church folk. In more clinical terms, we believe that a freak is really a person battling a sexual addiction. Sex addicts use sex like an alcoholic uses alcohol, as an anesthetizing drug that allows them to escape from their lives, if only temporarily.[1]

Even though it is not discussed commonly, sexual addictions are prevalent. The National Council on Sexual Addictions and Compulsivity says it gets about fifty e-mails and thirty to forty phone calls each week from people seeking help for themselves or a loved one.[2]

What do believers do when their sexuality spirals out of their control and into the realm of freak? What if you are driven beyond your control to do things that you know are not right? What if your mind is flooded with hounding, obsessive thoughts that compel you to do something over and over and over again? For example, do you ever wonder whether you turned off the iron before you left the house? Suppose that nagging question grew stronger and stronger, refusing to leave your mind? The only way to stop it is to go home to check the iron. This is what a compulsion is, and in the lives of sex addicts the compulsions are much stronger and they consume their lives. "The compulsion, this virtually irresistible urge to repeat a behavior again and again—regardless of the immediate harm it can cause or its long-range consequences—overrides the addict's logical thinking, moral judgment, and even the strongest desire not to do the compulsive behavior."[3]

Laughed at, talked about, and dismissed for decades as nymphomaniacs, sexaholics, perverts, and weirdos, sex addicts deserve God's grace like the rest of us.

∽ Case 1 ∾

The first person who came forward was a veteran churchman, with all the respect and honor of his church resting on his shoulders. In his secret life, he took it all off.

On a cloudy fall afternoon, he stood at the corner of a quiet city park, leaning against the bus stop signpost, brimming with anticipation for meeting and impressing women. "I know that at least one will come by who sees me and wants me," he thought to himself. Eventually two female joggers ran in his direction. His anticipation skyrocketed. "They wanted me sexually," he thought to himself with confidence. When the joggers were at arm's length, he swung open his coat to expose his nude body. The women screeched and ran away even faster, upset and sobbing. He sprinted to his car and sped across town to his church—he had to teach Bible study that evening.

Meet Daniel, one part saint, one part freak. He is an unassuming, peaceful-looking man in his mid-40s. Balding and slightly chubby, Daniel is a shoe shiner at a downtown mall. At church, he is Mr. Everything for this mid-size congregation. He teaches the men's Bible study class, serves as an armor-bearer to his pastor, and leads the church's scouting troop. He is loved by all and considered God-fearing and gentlemanly. With his starched white shirt, black pants, and loafers, Daniel is an icon of what a Christian man should be. Daniel is also the man in the park—a sex addict who fantasies about women and carries out those fantasies by exposing himself publicly.

"I get such a rush when I do it," Daniel explained. "It's like no other I've known. Drinks don't get me there. And my wife sure can't get me there. Chicks dig me and I dig them. I've got what they want and they don't have a problem asking me for it," he explained. "When I open my coat I feel like I am the King of the World. I just thought that if I only did it a few times that I'd be satisfied. I've got the corners of the parks around here memorized. I go there about six times a week. I'd probably go even more if I could squeeze it in between church and work," he speculated.

Daniel was raised in a violent home in a violent neighborhood. His dad never married his mother, and good thing that they didn't. They battled like gladiators. Dad was pissed off and high on that crack whenever he came over. He was always slapping me and Mom around. I could never do anything right. I hated him and I guess he hated me too. "With his own family, Daniel has created and maintains a similar relationship of hatred. He neglects them to lavish time at church and at the park. His wife knows about his sexual perversion, but feels powerless to stop him. His children only know him as angry and absent.

"I see no reason to stop," Daniel said firmly. "I keep the park thing separate from the church thing and the family thing. None of them ever mix. Sure the police have chased me a couple of times in their squad cars, and one time a cop on foot almost caught me. No matter. I got to do what I got to do. The high, the blast I get makes everything else shrink in comparison. I get the love that I need."

∽ Diagnosis ∾

"Daniel," I said, "you don't think that you have a problem, but you do. The actions that you've described illustrate the classic example of a sex addict."

> The overwhelming urge to partake in [sex], the utter disregard for the consequences that inevitably occur, and the inability to stop—no matter how sincerely you want to stop or how desperately you try.[4]

"There is an element of delusion there, too. The women that you see walking around are *not* after you. That's all in your mind, as is common for sex addicts. It's part of the sickness. When you flash your body at women, you get a thrill, while the women are terrified. You get a high, while they get horror. It's not a connection for them like it is for you.

"Your thoughts and fantasies about sex have gotten out of control and are now controlling you," I continued. "Lust is something that all of us battle. It's a part of humanity or the flesh as Paul said in Romans. But the uncontrolled lust has changed your behavior, thoughts, and feelings, and it's controlling every aspect of your life.[5]

"Your church seems to revolve around you, your extensive leadership roles and your image. They see the good in you, and it is there. I celebrate that part of you. The good part must win in this battle. Maybe you are spreading yourself too thin, because you haven't seen how detrimental the bad part is."

> Sex addicts relentlessly drive themselves to be good employees, good spouses, good parents, and good citizens, yet they draw a complete blank when trying to figure out what constitutes good behavior.[6]

∽ Prescription ∾

"You can't be an upstanding man of God for a few hours and then go flash your bare body to strange women," I told him firmly. "Your family is going neglected because you spend time with your addiction. And the congregation is completely hoodwinked. You are going to have to admit your sin before you can begin the healing.

"Cleaning up an addiction to anything, whether it is drugs, shopping, or sex, is a long, involved process. It's clear as glass to me that you've got two lives going on at once, but not to you. Denial is standing in your way to recovery.[7] Some of the forms of denial are minimizing the problem, blaming, rationalizing the problem, intellectualizing, diversion, or hostility.[8] You've used them all.

"Only when you admit that you have a problem can the

healing begin. Pray and ask the Lord to show you the error of your ways."

∞ **Case 2** ∞

Freaks can be male or female. Women are not immune to sexual sins and the compulsion to do them over and over and over. Katherine's story was equally as compelling as Daniel's. Like him, she was not a freak to be laughed at, but a lost soul, needing to find her way home.

Katherine came to kneel at the altar during services, with her face already drenched in tears. The pastor looked at her and smiled. He was happy she was there. She was a major tither. Her financial contributions alone kept the church in the black. Her name was lifted up and celebrated at that church, because she was a woman who feared and loved the Lord.

Katherine bowed her head and prayed, "God, I'm glad to be here. It's been a while, but you know where I've been. Lord, do something with me," she whispered to God. "I am about to lose my job. I can't keep this up. Keep me away from the men. I know I am wrong. Stop me from going to those places. I want this hell to end now," she pleaded.

Katherine, 38, is a top-notch national executive vice president of sales for a Fortune 500 firm—and she's on the verge of being fired. Her job is like a pressure cooker, with its endless demands to produce more and more revenue. The nonstop travel itinerary and cutthroat competition from co-workers has her always looking over her shoulder and watching her back. She is drowning. The late-night meetings and early-morning sales conferences have ruled out any opportunity to meet a meaningful man. She is lonely all the time. Things at the office are slipping. The high revenues are going to the other co-workers she always exceeded in the firm. She was passed over for the top sales award that she's always won. She's frayed and frantic.

To combat the excruciating stress of climbing up the corporate ladder, Katherine the corporate star and church contributor is also a freak. She delves into sexual fantasies that command the same time and energy she needs to stay number one at the firm. She's up until the wee hours of the morning surfing porn sites, masturbating, and fantasizing about her man. About twice a week, Katherine gets into her Jaguar and cruises the crack houses for a man to take home for the night. Any man will do.

"I think about men a lot. I can't seem to stop myself. Every week I promise myself that I will not go back to that street, but there I am," Katherine admitted. "The images and sensations race around and intensify in my mind and I like it. I think about them and not about this hellhole of a job that I have. The people here are strangling me. I need a way to balance all of this. The men help me," she said matter of factly.

Katherine grew up in an ultrastrict religious home—the breeding ground for sex addicts, say the therapists who treat them:

> The vast majority of sex addicts we treat were brought up in strictly religious homes of various denominations, and the attitudes about sexuality passed down to them by their parents were based on conservative religious teachings. By the time these addicts reached adulthood, they had been toughly indoctrinated in extremely restrictive beliefs about sexuality.[9]

"Any sexual expression from holding hands to kissing was labeled bad," she recalled. She was called a "dirty girl" when her parents found the harmless "do you like me?" notes that elementary school sweethearts send to each other. Her punishment was no television for a month. When her parents saw her kissing a boy at church after junior high choir practice, she was forced to quit the choir. "I felt the pleasure of attraction to boys, but the guilt came with it too, and the mixture of guilt and pleasure is what I feel to this day. My parents told me that I was worthless and that I was going to hell. And since I was going there anyway, I decided to keep on having fun. But I have had enough of this. I want out," she said.

∞ **Diagnosis** ∞

Katherine is a sex addict. Her actions tell her and the world that she holds a low opinion of herself, has a desire to escape from or to suppress unpleasant emotions, and has difficulty coping with stress.[10] Her addiction is seen in her obsession with porn sites and in her one-night stands with the male strangers that she picks up as she cruises the streets of drug-infested areas. Although she is educated, obviously accomplished, and has a relationship with God, her addiction is out of control. She is risking her life and her career with this behavior.

"Risking your job is a red flag that we all can see, Katherine—but can you see it?" I asked. "If you can throw all that you've worked for away for strangers and porn Internet sites, you are an addict. This addiction has turned you inside out. Certainly the men that you sleep with make you feel even worse. By going from man to man in your search for the ultimate high, you've opened yourself up to any number of potential deadly consequences. Some of your behavior may be in response to your strict upbringing. The message that you received is that sex was a taboo topic, a dirty topic, and as you grew up, you probably assumed that your sexual development and curiosity were signs of perversion.[11]

"The Good News is that you are a worthwhile, worthy, and wonderful woman. You have a lot to offer to your God, to yourself, to your job, as well as to a credible man when he comes around."

∞ Prescription ∞

The most effective way for addicts to finally acknowledge what is going on in their lives is for them to hit rock bottom. Katherine may be there, or about to reach it at any moment. She needs to turn off the negative tapes from her childhood, and get some help. Sexaholics Anonymous, Sex Addicts Anonymous, or Sex and Love Addicts Anonymous will offer a twelve-step way out.

Here is the first step: Admit that you are powerless over lust—that your life has become unmanageable. Of course, we all prefer to think that we do have control over our own lives, and especially over our actions in areas as sensitive as sexuality and personal relationships. Therefore, we find it not only difficult but also discouraging to admit powerlessness over compulsive behavior.[12]

We ended this Love Clinic asking God to protect us from ourselves: *No weapon that is formed against you will prosper* (Isaiah 54:17).

Let us pray

Dear God,

We are struggling with issues and concerns that require Your strength and might. We cannot make it on our own. We are helpless without Your divine might. Be our leader and guide us out of this time of distress.

Amen

Chapter 18

MY BABY'S DADDY

The halting stride of the petite 14-year-old girl moving toward the pulpit was painful to watch. The tense congregation knew what she was going to say once she reached her destination. Her hands wringing, her head bowed, and her abdomen extended, this young saint was an illustration of every believer's nightmare, a pregnant teenage daughter. And because it was the pastor's daughter who was pregnant, the church nearly had a conniption.

It was assumed at the most, and prayed for at the least, that his daughter would be immune to the trap of teen pregnancy. In their eyes, the young woman had shamed her family and her church. So she was marched to the front of the church, and was made to apologize for the sins she committed and the dishonor she brought before God and to her family. While her tearful confession gushed forth, the baby's father, the son of the trustee board chair, wanted to stand with her and admit his duplicity. But he thought it best to lower his head and keep quiet. After all, he was just the baby's daddy.

Who is the real culprit here?

A. The pregnant teen who will be raising her baby without its father.

B. The baby's father, who decided not to get involved.

C. The baby's grandparents, who never talked with their daughter or son about sex.

D. The congregation that never taught its young people what God says about sexual relations and abstinence?

E. All of the above?

The answer is *E*. We are *all* responsible. Yet the greater portion of prevention is in the hands of the adults. We must teach our young right from wrong by thought, word, and deed.

Having babies is a status symbol in many neighborhoods across America, and the more you have it seems the cooler you are. Apparently there is a lot of cool going around; America boasts the highest teen pregnancy rate among developed nations.[1] Some teens cannot help themselves. They are mimicking the adults in their midst, and the video stars and athletic heroes and heroines. They did not create this sexually explicit culture, but they are forced to live in it.

When the value of interdependence is spurned, the sacredness of sexual unions is trashed, and the notion of forming a family unit meets hostility, the self-destruction of our youth is eminent. This epidemic of teen pregnancy should have sounded an alarm in churches everywhere. Unfortunately, many churches are content to sit and watch the pregnancy parade waddle by, Sunday after Sunday. Whispering and pointing at them does not change a thing. But change can happen. These teens' best weapon is knowledge of themselves and their Jesus. Specifically, knowledge of their sexual selves, the God-inspired responsibility of that sexual self, and why the formation of healthy relationships is indispensable.

Proverbs 22:6 tells us, *Train up a child in the way he should go, even when he is old he will not depart from it.* In the context of sex education, this kind of training makes some church folk leave the room in a huff. We Christians are historically uneasy about articulating our sexuality. The uneasiness produces an anxiety that manifests itself in shame, embarrassment, and confusion. I've seen congregates squirm in their chairs and contort their faces when the mere suggestion of church-based, teen sex education is raised. Yet one look at the rate of teen pregnancy in America and it's clear that the young people are not uncomfortable with the idea of sex. Our silence is their green light.

∽ Case 1 ∽

"Don't follow me," said Lashan, a smiling 16-year-old who lives with her infant daughter in a church-operated shelter for teen mothers. "I made wrong choices, and now I am living them out. I did not intend to get pregnant. You know, it just happened. My mother could not afford to take in me and my child. She is barely making it herself. And my baby's daddy says it's not his. So it's just the two of us." Lashan is only a teenager, but she has the appearance of a much older woman. The father of her child is a 25-year-old man.

Some girls begin to look more grown-up and potentially more sexual at an earlier age others. Since they appear more womanly, their emotional maturity is assumed to be equal to their physical maturity. More is expected of them as sexually mature teens, when in reality they may still be little girls.[2]

"I'm glad that I found this church shelter. They helped me find a job, finish high school, and learn to take care of my daughter. Despite it all, God is good. It's going to be all right," she said with confidence. "I know I'm getting a job soon. One day we'll be living in a house and everything.

"I admit, I made some crazy choices in my life. I chose to skip school, to get high, and to lay down with a guy that I *knew* did not love me. He barely speaks to me and his child now," she said. "Now I am paying the price for what I did. Life ain't fair, is it? Is God mad at me?"

◌⊃ Diagnosis ◌⊃

"Lashan," I said, "you are a survivor. You have come through the storm of pregnancy and abandonment by the baby's father, now you face the storm of raising the child alone on a low salary and in public housing. If I had my choice for you, it would not have been like this. Yet studies tell us that teen mothers have a higher chance of living in poverty.

"Sometimes young women your age, opt to have a baby because they want something of their own," I explained. "The studies tell us that four out of ten teenage girls in the U.S. still become pregnant before age 20.[3]

"Our world is filled with a sense of brokenness. For some girls, a baby fills the void and gives them comfort. I am sorry that your baby's daddy has chosen not to be a part of his child's life. But please do not disrespect your baby's father. Your daughter should not grow up in the anger that you have for him. This may poison both of you and keep you from developing positive relationships in the future.

"Confession is good for the soul, and it is a plus that you see the error of your ways. God is not mad at you; God is simply allowing you to lie in the bed you made. Your foolish actions hurled you out of girlhood and into womanhood swiftly. Yet you seem strong, and I believe you and your baby will be fine," I added.

∞ Prescription ∞

As I told Lashan, the future can be bright if you get on the right path and stay there. I urged her to do three things.

1. Get control of your body and your mind. Pray and ask God to gain control over your sexual self. In our society, sex is used to sell everything from cars to pencils. This oversaturation of sex impacts our minds and causes us to seek sex as a means of personal validation, or to prove that we are OK. You are OK—you are a great person without having sex. If you can't live without sex, please use contraception.

2. Set some goals for yourself and your baby and work toward them. Studies tell us that "something for which to defer immediate gratification is an essential part of ado-

lescent growth and self-development. Setting goals requires a focus on something intangible. For teens achieving the exact goal they state may not be as important to their sexuality as learning self-discipline and recognizing that their efforts can move them toward their goals."[4]

3. Get involved in a support group for teenage moms. You need to be undergirded, nurtured, loved, and guided by positive, progressive people. Even though you are a mother, you are still developing into a woman. You need a safe place to process thoughts, set personal boundaries, and grow. Dr. Gail Wyatt, a noted therapist and researcher on Black women's issues, offers a helpful guide to young women and their decision-making called *CARE*.

C. Consistency in behavior over time, maturity, communication, trust, and mutual respect are necessary in any relationship before sex is considered.

A. Always remember to evaluate if you are dating someone who can be a life partner.

R. Responsibility begins with you.

E. Each time you consider sex, think about the consequences to you and your future.[5]

◈ Case 2 ◈

There are two sides to every story. Too many teen pregnancy programs start and end with the young women. There are young men also involved in this formula. They must be heard and helped, too.

James, a tall, husky 15-year-old who looked more like 20, came forward. Despite the fact that he was raised in the church,

James is sexually active and proud of it. Recent surveys tell us that James is not alone:

> While sexual activity has decidedly declined among teens, for those under 15 it has not. There is a 15 percent increase in students who say they have had sex before age 13.[6]

"All this talk about being a baby's daddy is not what I want to hear," he said. "My homies and me are about getting some. Why shouldn't we? If females want to give it, we will take it. Availability is the name of the game. I don't care about afterward; I care about how I feel when I'm there. When it's over, it's over. Yeah, a girl at church has told people that her baby is mine. She's lying. I was with her once, and it wasn't even good," he declared. Often young men like James father children and feel a financial obligation to the mother, but feel attracted to other girls. Many get confused and depressed.[7]

"I don't think I'm doing anything wrong. Most of the grown folk do the same thing, too," said James, who lives with his parents in a middle-class neighborhood. "I watch them at church and everywhere else. I'm just starting a little early. Anyway, what does this have to do with God? I see two separate issues."

∽ Diagnosis ∽

"James," I said, "I want you to know that God loves you and God is always involved in whatever we do with ourselves. We cannot separate our bodies into zones where God cannot enter or have control. The Bibles tells us to live lives of sexual purity while we are single. You can still be a cool guy without having sex.

"Brother, you are heading down a dangerous pathway fast, because you are allowing your genitals to make your decisions.

"They don't have that much clout. In the words of my good friend, *Essence* magazine relationship columnist Dr. Gwen Grant Goldsby, 'an erection is not an emergency. Many brothers consider an erection to be some kind of emergency. They say things like there's a fire in the cellar. That means they want somebody to put it out as soon as possible because the alarm has sounded.'[8]

"Yes, I am sure that your body is telling you that a sexual alarm has sounded, but before you continue on, stop and pray and ask God for help," I said.

∽ Prescription ∾

"James, God has something better planned for you. It begins with you closing your fly and opening your heart to being transformed in the name of Jesus. First of all, God wants you to understand that women are not sex objects. Despite what you see others doing to them or with them, follow the way that leads to treating them with respect. Please consider becoming sexually nonactive or abstinent. If you can't do that yet, by all means use contraception," I urged.

"I suggest that you step back and look at the direction you are headed in. If you do not alter your path, you will wind up like too many brothers we know—with babies all over town."

The baby-maker [is] a guy who does not want to be inconvenienced with safe sex or birth control. He convinces women to have his baby just because it seems like the thing to do. He brags about his children; sometimes he may even go to visit one of them for a bit, but he does not love them the way their mother does. To him they are just showcase babies for him to show off and prove his manhood.[9]

"I recommend that you find a mentor—a man who can spend time with you and offer you direction about your life. Please become active in a church youth group that is not afraid to tackle the real problems that today's youth are facing."

We concluded this session with the young people agreeing that they could tap into the power of Jesus to resist sexual temptation, as found in Philippians 4:13: *I can do all things through Him who strengthens me.*

Let us pray
> Dear God,
> We pray for teen parents everywhere. Give them the strength they need to be positive, godly parents. Let them know that they can make it with Your unchanging hand.
> Amen

Chapter 19

THE INVISIBLE LIFE CAN BE SEEN, IF WE OPEN OUR EYES

Carl loves men, and Katrina loves women. Sitting side by side in the pew perpetuating a loving marriage is hard work for both of them. They execute this heterosexual prevarication every Sunday morning for appearance's sake. After all, she is chair of the women's mission board, and he is a respected deacon. But, when the sanctified crowd is not around, Carl and Katrina shift gears and become who they understand God made them to be, homosexual Christians. They feel that the church denies their rights to authenticity. So they maintain two separate and un-equal lives. They love the church, yet they love who they are, too. The Scriptures say, *the truth will make you free* (John 8: 32). But in the minds of these two tithing, Scripture-quoting, homosexual Christians, speaking the truth would not set them free. It would subject them to the hellified judgment of fellow church members.

Homophobia is a rampant illness of the church. This anxiety manifests itself in a number of ways. Some churches refuse to recognize the large numbers of homosexual men and women in their congregations. Gay men and lesbian women are an active part of nearly every church in America, from the pulpit to the maintenance department. They serve the church while in the closet or out in the open.

Cornel West has observed the ways that gay persons have always been a part of the American community:

> [W]hen I was growing up, most people knew that, let's say, the brother who played the organ in the church was a gay brother. People would say, oh, that's so and so's child. You know, he's that way. And they'd just keep moving. There wasn't an attempt to focus on his sexuality; he was an integral part of the community. It wasn't a matter of trying to target him and somehow pester him or openly publicly degrade him . . . [1]

Some churches use the scripture to support their homophobic attitudes. They interpret Romans 1:26 as the reason that homosexuals should be sent to hell. The verse reads, *For this reason God gave them over to degrading passions; for their women exchanged the natural function for that which is unnatural, and in the same way also the men abandoned the natural function of the woman and burned in their desire for one another.*

Others say they should be accepted and treated with respect, because they were created homosexual and God created everything, based on Genesis 1:26, *Then God said, "Let Us make man in Our image, according to Our likeness."* Some say that the homosexual orientation is formed in the womb. But this sets up a heated debate, because some feel that homosexuality is acquired through experience. Christians find themselves wailing and screaming at each other over the issue.

Most pastors can preach on every issue under the sun except homosexuality. Their silence also muzzles the congregations in the face of a great opportunity for dialogue. However many pastors are afraid of splitting their congregation, or losing parishioners or income because of speaking out on this taboo subject.

∞ Case 1 ∞

The Love Clinic assembled a panel of homosexual Christians and asked them to share their sojourns in God's house. One gay brother, known only as B.L., a 36-year-old clothing store salesman, told his saga as a closeted gay man within the church. He grew up in a home that was not particularly religious, but many of the boys in his neighborhood attended church and he went with them. He went to church looking for shelter.

"I went to church looking for somebody to understand what I was going through," he said. "I've been like this all my life, and there was no one to talk to. My parents spent little time with me. They had three and four jobs. They were so into their money and status that I really did not matter," B.L. explained.

"I feel as though I have been an outcast inside the church all my life," he said. "I'm there every Sunday hoping to hear a word for me. The only word I hear is the minister telling me, and those like me, how dirty we are."

These words nearly destroyed B.L. as a youth. He received ridicule and condemnation at home, and he expected more from the church. The church's rejection made him feel that he was

worthless. "I tried to take myself out twice. There was no reason to keep on going with everyone lined up against me," he
said. "I used sleeping pills both times. My mom kept big bottles
of them in her bathroom closet," he confessed.

"No one knows what homosexuals experience in everyday
life," B.L. said. "I've been told that we've chosen this way of
life. I know this was not the case for me. I was not sexually
molested or traumatized in some way by a gay man. I just love
men and not women. I am now bitter at the church. I used to
enjoy going to church, but it is all now a facade. I often ask
myself, Where is all this love supposed to be? I am ready to
give up on Jesus and find me another lover for my soul."

∞ Diagnosis ∞

I told him, "Please don't give up on Jesus. Jesus is always the
answer. B.L., your disillusionment at the church is understand-
able. But Jesus never fails. The church is supposed to be the
place where we meet the saving grace of Jesus, but for many it
is a place of condemnation. Many church folk are caught in this
situation. They want to reach out to homosexual people, but
they fear the repercussion of embracing someone who is different. The irony is that Jesus teaches us to always reach out to
those around us who are different.

"The church's negative behavior has caused you to doubt
yourself or stop loving yourself. Your self-esteem has been damaged by the antics of church folk. You mentioned that you had
an especially painful time during your teen years. That's a lot
more common than you may know. Sometimes it helps to learn
that you are not the only one."

According to a report on youth suicide, "gay adolescents

were two to three times more likely than their peers to attempt suicide. The average age at the time of the first suicide attempt was 15.5 years. Almost half of them made their first attempt in the year that they first identified themselves as gay . . ."[2]

∞ Prescription ∞

As I urged B.L., I urge others like him to never give up on Jesus, no matter how angry you are with the church. There is a difference between church and God. And that difference should give you some peace of mind. More and more churches are opening their hearts and minds and are welcoming homosexual persons without fear.

Such churches are re-created congregations that are about the business of re-creating the way they approach being a caring community of faith and sharing the message of hope that such a re-created community has to offer.[3]

The problem is that "many people are fearful that if they proclaim God's radical grace, they will be seen as condoning any and all behavior. It's essential to separate the act of proclaiming grace and welcome to a hurting world from the act of discerning and maintaining ethical standards in human community. Both are important, but they are different tasks."[4]

Most of all, Jesus is the ultimate judge; you should work out your salvation with Him in mind.

∞ Case 2 ∞

Another voice from the homosexual community came in the form of Tracey, a 45-year-old lesbian, who is a registered nurse at an area hospital. She is a tall woman with salt-and-pepper shoulder-length hair. Tracey has "come out," or publicized her homosexual lifestyle. She lives with Kaye, her mate of fifteen years. They have a comfortable life together, but it is separate from the community and the church.

"I don't think I can ever go back to church, even though I was raised there," she said. "There is so much pain there. Yes, the singing is good and the preaching is good, but there is not a place for a lesbian in the traditional church."

Tracey's sexual orientation took on the invisible label because of the harsh reaction of family to her lifestyle. "I came out as a lesbian while I was in college," she said. "It started with crushes on girls in elementary school. It continued into high school. I thought everybody was like me until my first real love relationship. When word got out around church that two girls were kissing in the Sunday school building, it was over for me. Kids hit me, spit on me.

"Even though I prayed hard all the time, the church was a battleground. There was no one to help me. My dad was the pastor, and he was not having a gay daughter. He was harder on me than the church kids. And today, he barely speaks to me, only to tell me that I am a sinner. I lost my family when I embraced my identity," Tracey said.

∞ Diagnosis ∞

"Tracey, your pain is the loss of family. Family rejection is brutal for anyone gay or straight," I said. "We all want the love that comes from our parents and siblings. Your father's denial of you as a daughter is probably like a knife in your heart, but you have to be who you are."

Gay and lesbian persons and their families "are caught in a trap and are usually tortured from each side of the dilemma. Almost universally they deeply desire an open and honest relationship with their parents . . . Yet they are usually very afraid of the family member's reactions; what they will think, feel or do."[5]

Homosexuals may experience depression, sorrow, and even pressure to pass or pretend that they are not gay. Our community enjoys pretending or insisting that lesbians are not there. As one lesbian writer has commented,

> We. . . are still walking around the edge of the room, trying to ignore the elephant sitting in the middle. I think many would prefer me to pass in the community. For some, I can be a lesbian in what I imagine as my dark, secret world, but when I'm in the community, the message to me is: don't bring that mess.[6]

∽ Prescription ∾

Many gay and lesbians may feel they have to choose between their lifestyle and their parents' approval. But it is important to realize what the family may be going through. There are five stages that are experienced when a homosexual comes out to their family.

> Their first reaction is anger because there is a sense of being betrayed. The second reaction is shock and denial. No you're not. We did not raise you to be like this, they say. The third reaction is yearning. The parents yearn for their son or daughter

to return to the way they were. The parents may feel that their child has died and they want to see him or her again. The fourth stage is transition, parents begin to let go of their dreams and attempt to see their son or daughter more realistically. The final stage, resolution-reconciliation is not always reached. For some parents, their final stage is the failure of the transitional stage to be a transition, and therefore they are stuck with their feelings of sadness, incompleteness, pain, and disillusionment with their child, etc.[7]

Your family may be stuck, in their reaction to the news, but you press on with your life. Don't let their poison be your problem. In the midst of this struggle you will benefit from a strong support system, and a faith in God that is unshakable. Keep on seeking God's face, and you will survive this storm.

This Love Clinic, at the least, opened the eyes of the heterosexual congregates to the struggles of our homosexual brothers and sisters. It also gave us the nerve to keep the channels of communication open. Victory in the 21st century for Christians hinges on civil dialogue. The invisible life can be seen if we open our eyes.

We concluded this Love Clinic with confidence in the unity of Christ to find a common ground:

For even as the body is one and yet has many members, and all the members of the body, though they are many, are one body, so also is Christ. *For by one Spirit we were all baptized into one body, whether Jews or Greeks, whether slaves or free, and we were all made to drink of one Spirit. For the body is not one member, but many* (Corinthians 12:12–14).

Let us pray

Dear God,

In the midst of conflict we pause to praise You as our common denominator. May our shared love of You bind us closer. May our mutual ministry of service connect us despite the differences. We know You are able.

Amen

Chapter 20

YOU CAN RUN, BUT YOU CAN'T HIDE FROM AIDS

Look into the face of AIDS and see a well-dressed, educated, heterosexual person with a Bible in her hand, sitting in the pew to your left. To your right is also the face of AIDS, in an elementary schoolchild with a ponytail and a mischievous smile. The face of AIDS may also be in front of you, in the pastor preaching up a storm. AIDS is no longer the "white gay disease"—it is an epidemic. The never-ending stereotype of AIDS survivors makes them monsters, not the people with whom you share the Holy Communion. As much as some would like to ignore it, AIDS affects us all—old or young, male or female, gay or straight, sinner or saint.

The denial of AIDS is tied to homophobia. As long as AIDS was hitting the gay white community, heterosexuals, women, and people of color could ignore it. Now it is where we all live.

It is in our churches, and many of us are running scared. For example, Mary's hands still tremble as she reflects on her encounter with AIDS, in the form of an HIV-infected choir member. Once Mary was an active member of her church, but now she spends her Sunday mornings sitting on her back porch reading novels.

"When I heard what he had, I could not continue to sing in the choir or function around him," she said. "People like that should stay to themselves, and not come to mess up the church. It's too dangerous. No one else agreed, so I left. I feel safer here than at that contaminated church."

This is a unkind story, but it illustrates how some church folk have become alarmed and afraid of what they do not understand. Fear makes us do strange things and ask even stranger questions: What if I catch something? Well, how did they get it in the first place? Isn't AIDS just God's way of punishing sinful folk?

The church should be doing what Jesus did. He reached out to people in need, regardless of their station or situation. In the book of Luke 10:30–37, Jesus teaches us with a parable of a man who was beaten, robbed, and left for dead. As the man lay bleeding, two religious leaders approached him, saw his wounds, said nothing and kept going. Finally, a Samaritan, the most despised of ethnic groups, approached the man. The Samaritan stopped, bandaged his wounds, and took care of him. The Samaritan did more than offer roadside assistance. He carried the wounded man to an inn and paid for his accommodations. Jesus admonished his followers to *go and do the same.*

What this says to us today is "how we treat people in need

is more important than social and religious respectability, and the person in need is my neighbor, and I am a neighbor when I help someone in need."[1]

∞ Case 1 ∞

Clara didn't want to tell her story, but she could not hold her peace. "I had to sit down when my doctor told me that I had contracted HIV," she recalled. "I told him, look that can't be. I am 67 years old. I am not funny. I do not mess around with other women or other men. I've been married to the same man for 45 years, and never was unfaithful. I don't have nobody's AIDS. You are wrong! The doctor told me that he believed that I was a faithful wife and that I was hetero-whatever-you-call-it, straight, but he said that I had contracted the disease anyhow. I whispered a prayer to God—let it be a mistake.

"I drove home so fast from the doctor's office that it seemed like I was the pilot of a jet instead of my little Toyota. I ran in the house and asked Milt, my husband, if he'd been fooling around, because I've got something. He denied it for two days, but eventually he got scared and went to see his doctor. He 'fessed up months later that the women he was seeing on the side gave it to him."

Clara was a graying woman who was aging well. Her disease threw a wrench in her retirement plans. She was active with her sorority and another civic social women's club. All of that was down the drain now. "Now what does an old woman like me do with herself and AIDS?" she asked. "I'm supposed to be retired without a care in the world. And here I am having to fight a new battle. Where do I go for support? I certainly can't go to the church. They are the last bunch to talk to. The last time a member confided in the pastor, he preached about her business the next Sunday. What could the church do? How could they help me?"

↬ Diagnosis ↫

I told her, "Clara, you have been through a lot in a short period of time. AIDS, the betrayal by your spouse, and the reality that your life will never be the same. Everyone needs somebody or someplace to rest their burdens. The lack of a support group for you at this time means that you may experience alienation."

> The experience of alienation elicits feelings of isolation, abandonment, and despair. These feelings inevitably arise when a person is deprived of social interaction and community. When family members no longer can be supportive, when friends fail to visit, when society stigmatizes, and communities exclude people with AIDS, the result is alienation and despair.[2]

"Your husband's infidelity is the major blow that started your trials and tribulations. Your relationship with him may be uncertain. No one can blame you for being angry with him. He endangered your life by his cheating ways. Now the both of you are paying the price for his indiscretion."

↬ Prescription ↫

Anyone faced with a life-threatening or life-changing event will experience a range of emotions. Often these feelings come in stages (although not everyone experiences all the stages or in the same order).

The first stage is denial. People living with AIDS can't believe that they have it. They think that it must be some kind of mistake. The next stage is rage and anger. (That's where Clara may be right now.) Of all the people in the world, why would God put this on you? Next, the person begins to bargain with God for healing in return for promised actions—if you heal me God, I'll serve your people. Depression comes next, as they grieve what could have been. Acceptance is the final stage. It is not necessarily a happy stage or an unhappy one. Acceptance is more of a resignation that they cannot change what is.[3]

I explained to Clara, "Your relationship with your spouse is pivotal. If you choose to remain with him, the two of you can form a team. Yet if you cannot go forward with him because your trust has been shattered, you are strong enough to face this. Either way you will need a support team. If your church is not the place, look elsewhere."

⚬⚬ Case 2 ⚬⚬

Vincent is a 41-year-old father of two who is living with AIDS, which he contracted from a blood transfusion. His wife contracted the disease from him, and died from AIDS complications. He is open about his health condition with his church and had a positive experience there.

"The church is a place of hope. We should not give up on it. My church family rallied around me when I told them of my illness. They look after my children when I am too weak, they even take me to the doctor's office for my visits. Most of all," he added, "they cover me in prayer. It makes the difference."

Prior to her death, Vincent and his wife were active members of the church. Their faith was often mentioned by the pastor as something others could aspire to. "My concern is that I feel like God has abandoned me. I just don't sense the connection that I used to. Has God turned his back on me?"

Diagnosis

I told Vincent, "I praise God for your church, and the way they have rallied around you. They are a blessing. Obviously, they understand that we are responsible to each other no matter what. And their presence in your life is proof that God is not done with you.

"Asking if God has turned his back on you is logical. When trouble strikes it feels like we are all alone. The greater the intensity of the trouble, the less likely we are to hear God calling our name. Believe me, Vincent, God is still calling your name and still has blessings in store for you. You must have faith. The presence of the AIDS virus in your body probably does depress you, but never forget the power of God in your soul. Believers are known for their joy in the midst of sorrow. Hold your head high."

Prescription

"Vincent, I suggest that you make use of your positive relationship with your church to become an educator about AIDS. More and more church people need to see and meet the real face of AIDS—which is you. AIDS is a tragedy; yet there is within the crisis the inherent opportunity for AIDS to be the agent of healing and bridge of hope to the God of all comfort and light. Chronic illness can lead to redemption. Suffering can force us to search the depths of our souls where we find strength, hope, and God's healing presence."[4]

We ended this session on AIDS with praise to God for victory in spite of challenges, using as our guide Psalm 27:1: *The Lord is my light and my salvation; whom shall I fear? The Lord is the defense of my life; whom shall I dread?*

Let us pray

Dear Lord,

You are greater than any disease. Focus our eyes on the provision and not the problem. Don't let our fears separate us one from another. Keep the devil from splitting churches, families, and communities. Let us find unity in You.

Amen

Chapter 21

⁂

WHEN LOVING YOU HURTS ME

Blackened eyes, loosened teeth, and bruised bodies limp into sanc-tuaries every Sunday morning. Makeup, turtlenecks, scarves, and hats attempt to camouflage the wounds. Yet the hurt is there. In many instances it will continue, because the beaters and the beaten are trapped in an obscene dance, where a whack means love and domination means affection. They, like the rest, come to hear the Word, give God some praise, and receive a blessing.

Violence against women is interwoven into the fabric of who we are as Americans. Staggering statistics tell us that this is a serious national problem. According to reports there are "3.9 million women who are physically abused by their husbands or live-in partners per year."[1] "Nearly one-third of American women (31 percent) report being physically or sexually abused by a husband or boyfriend at some point in their lives."[2]

Christians who punch, kick, and scratch other believers are, well, hard to envision, because we are taught that the love of Jesus conquers all. We are taught that prayer changes things. However, when Scripture-quoting mamas won't stop beating their children senseless with chairs, and sanctified husbands body-slam their wives down flights of stairs, doubts and questions arise about what God intended for relationships.

Church folk see, but don't acknowledge, the vestiges of domestic violence. The dangers of stepping into extreme relationships between adults or children makes one stop and count the costs. We shake our heads, and wag our tongues, saying, Why doesn't she just leave? I wouldn't take all of that! All the while, the fury rages on from one generation to the next.

One contributor to the violence is plain old confusion about what the Bible says concerning assault as a means of family control. Some Christians translate Scriptures such as Hosea 2:2, *For she is not my wife, and I am not her husband; And let her put away her harlotry from her face . . . or I will strip her naked And expose her as on the day when she was born*, as a guidebook for disciplining wayward wives. They reason that it's in the Bible so it must be God's will that husbands beat their wives.

∽ **Case 1** ∾

When Carl, a 37-year-old insurance executive, came forth, we assumed his testimony would be a confession of a batterer. It was not. This medium-build brother with a mustache and glasses revealed a side of domestic abuse that few knew existed: women batterers.

"This would be embarrassing for me, but it's too important

to keep to myself," he began. "My wife has an anger problem. She is the abuser in our home. She got it from her father. He terrorized her childhood, and now she can't or won't stop tearing up our family." Carl was referring to his wife, Nina, a forceful, no-nonsense woman. Carl and Nina met while in college. He was attracted to her work ethic and her focus on life and her career. After their three children were born, Nina's demeanor changed. She was diagnosed with a mental illness and given the appropriate medication. However, without the medication Nina is delusional and violent. She hits, slaps, and kicks her family when they do not follow her demands.

"What man can call for help when something like this is happening? I can't stop her," he stressed. "Over the 12 years of our marriage, I let her tear me down. I hate myself. I am not the same. I've tried to tell our pastor about it, but my wife is one of the top leaders of the church, and a prominent member of the prayer committee. No one would believe that she has two personalities."

The situation at home has become even more critical. When Carl announced his plans for a divorce, his wife held a gun to his head, demanding that he change his mind. Carl is anxious and has not been able to think clearly since then. "I stayed for the kids' sake. But what about my sake? I thought prayer was supposed to change this. How do I change her? Why is God doing this to me?" he asked.

∞ Diagnosis ∞

"Carl," I said, "I commend you for sharing your story without hesitation. The battered brothers of America also salute you. Your wife's violent mood swings have obviously damaged your self-worth and that of your children. Her words and actions, little by little, have chipped away at your self-image, which is why you seem very anxious and disoriented. Guilt and shame are common responses to abuse."

Many in this situation choose to pray for change, yet that is what keeps them trapped. Acceptance of the situation isn't a solution either, as condoning the behavior will also not produce change. Turning to God doesn't seem like an option either, because He seems to have turned away from the situation.

∽ Prescription ∾

"Carl, I do believe that the lives of you and your children may be in danger. I do not like to take chances with violent people who make threats. You and the children should get away from her as soon as possible."

Yet we know that when an abused spouse attempts to leave his abuser, that is the most dangerous time. Let me share the advice given to me from domestic violence shelters on how an abused person prepares to leave the abusive relationship. This is a partial list.

- Find a safe place where you and your children can go

- Decide who at work you will inform of your situation.

- When at work, if possible have someone screen your telephone calls.

- If at all possible, use a variety of routes to come and go from your own home.

- Develop a safety plan with your children for when you are not with them.

- Inform your child's school, day care, and other locations about who has permission to pick up your children.

- In case of an explosive incident, pack a bag and have it ready at a friends' or relative's house.

- Devise a code word to use with your children, family, friends, and neighbors when you need the police.[3]

∞ **Case 2** ∞

Rita began her story by emphasizing her accomplishments. "I finally escaped after fifteen years of hell," she said. "He beat the common sense out of me a long time ago. That's why I stayed with him. I thought I was supposed to be hit all the time. I felt that I wasn't pretty, so I allowed stuff to happen. We never bothered to get married, and I'm glad we didn't." Rita invested fifteen years in a relationship with a popular, yet violent man who was a political leader in her city. The two were an attractive couple. No one ever suspected there was violence in the relationship, but friends and family always wondered why the two never married.

"We began dating in high school," said Rita, a 38-year-old dentist. "He was the star athlete, and I was the head cheerleader. Everyone said we looked good together, so I thought we'd be good together. We have not been good together. But back then I did not know what to expect in a relationship. I was just a kid in love," she recalled.

"The violence started slowly; first he'd slap me when I disagreed with him. Then he'd punch me if I gave my opinion. I'd be shoved when things did not go his way. The next thing I knew, I'd have a black eye for anything—late dinner, a bad hair day, rain, anything! The next time it was a bruise on my back or a cracked wrist. Every time he'd apologize and buy me something. I enjoyed the gifts, and quickly forgave him, until the next time. Eventually he had me in the palm of his hand. I was in too deep to see my way out.

"I couldn't tell anybody," she said. "My family has never been there for me, and I don't have many friends. I knew that I could not report him to his pastor," she continued. "He was a big giver and the pastor never bothered people like that. So one day I told him that I'd had enough. He must have felt the same way; he never tried to see me again. Why do I still love him? Why do I think about him all the time? If I could just get a new man in my life, it would be great."

∞ Diagnosis ∞

"Rita," I said, "congratulations on your freedom! Exodus from that abuse required courage. You are brave and smart. Your ex-boyfriend indoctrinated you with violence for a long time, and you learned to accept it. Eventually the abuse symbolized love for you. You still have feelings for him because many survivors like yourself suffer from a sense of ambivalence because you loved and hated the man all at once. The conflicting feelings can be confusing and can cause the survivor to feel crazy. Additionally, others often deny the abuse. When what is seen or experienced as true in oneself is contradicted by others, feelings of craziness result."[4]

∞ **Prescription** ∞

After ending an abusive relationship the survivor must take time for herself. Now is the time to reach out to family or friends, if they are available. If you don't have family or friends, reach out to a community or a support network of trustworthy people.

Time is needed before entering into a new relationship. A survivor needs time to develop a relationship with herself and take a break from the demands of a couple relationship. Spend a year giving the emotional scars time to heal and use the time to reflect on what the future will bring.

We closed this session of the Love Clinic with the power of positive thinking, as found in Philippians 4:8: *Whatever is true, whatever is honorable, whatever is right, whatever is pure, whatever is lovely, whatever is of good repute, if there is any excellence and if anything worthy of praise, dwell on these things.*

Let us pray
  Dear God,
  Thank You for being my shelter in the time of storms. Thank You for loving me when I could not love myself. Heal me from the inside out. Only You can restore the wounds of my soul and my body. Cover me with peace that restores.
  Amen

Chapter 22

WHY DOES IT HURT SO BAD?

Pain, sorrow, and despair will come into your life at some time or another. That's why Jesus said, in John 16:33, *In the world you have tribulation, but take courage; I have overcome the world.*

When suffering comes, we need to ask ourselves will we handle it or will it handle us? As Yale sister theologian Shawn Copeland has written,

> Suffering can maim, wither, and cripple the heart, or to quote Howard Thurman, it can be a spear of frustration transformed into a shaft of light . . . From some women and men, suffering extracts bitter venom. From still others, suffering squeezes a delicious ironic spirit and tough laughter. Consider the Gullah (woman's) proverb: Ah done been in sorrow's kitchen and ah licked de pots clean.[1]

Sometimes the best thing to do is cry. Dr. Linda Hollies, in her book *Mother Goose Meets a Woman Called Wisdom* writes,

> There comes a time in the course of human events when tears are just plain necessary. Whether you are "together," "tough" or "bad," in periods of difficulty and pain you need to know how to cry. When you find yourself standing at the crossroads of disappointment and despair, it's no laughing matter. Then is the time for tears. When you arrive at the intersection of Sorrow's Boulevard and Suffering's Avenue, trying to figure out how to move, which direction to take, or how to choose which way you should go, sometimes all you can do is cry.[2]

The saying goes, "preach to the suffering, and you will never lack a congregation. There is a broken heart in every pew."[3]

The pain that accompanies relationship woes is excruciating. Pain at the hands of the one you thought loved you aches. Can a loved one pour gallons and gallons of ache into your heart?

∽ Case 1 ∾

Faith was an attractive, young woman with sorrow etched across her face. She said, "Dr. Patterson, I have one simple question. Is it possible to be raped by a loved one?" A hush raced across the sanctuary. Smiles instantly evaporated from the faces of our usually jovial crowd. This was getting serious.

"I am 24 years old and have two children," she explained.

"I have been in a relationship with a man for seven years. Four and a half of those seven years he was in prison. I stuck by his side, wrote, and visited him while he was incarcerated. We used to live together, but while he was in there I became a Christian and developed a relationship with the Lord. Recently, he was let out of prison and it became apparent to me that I had a deeply embedded soul tie with his man. He speaks my love language," Faith said, smiling.

This woman needed something to smile about. Her life to this point had been dismal. Her parents divorced while she was a baby, and she lived with a mother who did not want her. As a result, Faith continually searched for someone who would love her. "Last night for the first time in years we were face to face in a private home," she continued. "After being a single parent and having to carry the load for the last four and a half years it felt wonderful—even the thought of having some help. It has been years since anyone has held me, kissed me, or touched me. I kind of prided myself on being celibate for this long, and had promised the Lord I would not have sex with another man until I was married. And last night I wanted a touch, an act of affection, and I settled for a grope, a French kiss, and one 'I love you.'

"This would not be so terribly bad if it would have ended there," Faith said, with a voice choked with tears. "But eventually he did not heed to my No's. He is 6' 8" and 300 pounds. And it wasn't until I started crying profusely that he stopped. I feel violated, dishonored, unloved, discouraged, and like I have broken the covenant between my Lord and me," she sobbed. "He has apologized several times and his phone calls are without ceasing, and yet I love him. What in the world is wrong with me? My spirit knows that he is not a mighty man of valor and that he is not in the realm of my purpose—but what do I do? I don't want to call the police. He just got out of prison, and our children think that he is a super dad.

"He is the only man that has ever loved me even this much."

∾ Diagnosis ∾

I told her, "Faith, you are in a complex situation. Thank you so much for coming forward tonight. Someone that you love has demonstrated very unloving behavior toward you. In most instances the answer to your question would be simple—call the police. But the extenuating circumstances here cause me to pause and reflect on several factors."

First of all, Faith was the victim of rape. Specifically date rape or acquaintance rape:

> [Date rape is] forced, unwanted intercourse with a person you know. It is a violation of your body and your trust. It is an act of violence and it is a crime.[4] Experts tell us that as many as 90 percent of all rapes are never reported; in those that are reported, about 60 percent of the victims know their assailants.[5]

Date rape occurs for at least three major reasons:

1. Miscommunication—mixed signals, and no is erroneously believed to mean yes.

2. Socialization—men are taught to be aggressors and women are taught to be passive.

3. Changing sexual mores—men are allowed to have sexual feelings and act on them, but women are allowed to be sexual only when carried away with emotion.[6]

"Faith, there is a pervasive tendency of rape victims to blame themselves and feel guilty and confused. I am hearing confusion in your voice, and I see it on your face," I continued. "This man said he loved you, how could this happen? You may be very angry with yourself right now. All of this is the normal reaction.

"Much of the confusion stems from being a Christian. When a person of faith tries to move a notch higher, Satan comes along to knock us down. They call it 'new level new devil.' You were being true to the Word of God, and look at the result. You may be thinking, 'if I had not turned my life over to Christ, none of this would have happened,' " I counseled. "As a pastor I see this happen time and time again. The Lord wants us to improve, but Satan does not. This is a real life example of the reality, *For our struggle is not against flesh and blood, but against the rulers, against the powers, against world forces of this darkness* (Ephesians 6:11).

"Faith, from a clinical standpoint, rape experts tell us that the victims usually go through three definable stages of rape trauma syndrome: trauma, denial, and resolution.[7] The trauma stage means that you may have a fear of being alone, or a fear of men. You may be experiencing depression or you may experience physical problems such as headaches, stomachaches, or a diminished appetite. In the denial stage there is a desire to avoid the topic, to not want to talk about it, to put it behind you and get on with life. The final stage is resolution. In this stage you will begin to deal with your feelings, hopefully by talking it over with someone. And you will regain a sense of your self-control.[8]

"We need to examine the future of this relationship from a faith perspective. The fact that you are now a Christian, but were not one when the two of you first met and started a family, is crucial. Your new spiritual walk and new talk has caused friction in your relationship now. Due to your ties to Christ, your ties with your man are different. You will have to answer the pointed question about being unequally yoked. In 2 Corinthians 6:14 we read, *Do not be bound together with unbelievers; for what partnership has righteousness and lawlessness, or what fellowship has light and darkness?*

"When believers adopt the life of sexual abstinence, all types of temptations come their way. It was surely much easier to hold on to abstinence while he was behind bars, wasn't it? When the object of our sexual desire is absent we can sing the praises of God. We understand your struggle there, sister. We understand all of your struggles, Faith. They overlap and interface."

∞ Prescription ∞

"Faith, even though you believe that you are in love with his man, you must put the priority of safety for you and your children first," I said. "Any man who can sexually assault the woman that he loves is not safe to continue in a relationship with. If you continue on with him, you do so at your own risk."

There are four things that women in Faith's situation must do.

1. Forgive yourself and don't blame yourself. Forgiving yourself means that you let yourself off the hook. You give
   yourself permission to have fallen into difficulty and you
   accept your humanness. You must pardon yourself and
   love yourself in spite of this terrible act committed against
   you. Otherwise, you can go through life mentally kicking
   yourself for doing something so wrong.

   Forgiving yourself and not blaming yourself go hand in
   hand. Although the stage was set for the crime against
   Faith, she cannot hold herself totally at fault. Her man
   had the power to walk away when she said no and began
   to cry. She must not let him or anyone else pin this incident on her.

2. Forgive him, whether or not you get back together or you
   call the police. Don't carry around a lot of anger and rage
   at him forever. Yes, there will be some during the initial
   months of your healing. If you hold on to it beyond then,
   you give him and the act of violence too much power and
   authority in your life.

3. Write your attacker a letter telling him how you feel. The
   letter should have three parts: the factual account of what
   happened, a description of how the events made you feel,
   and an account of what you want to see happen next.
   Have this letter sent by certified mail. These letters "give
   the victim a sense of doing something constructive about
   the situation. It can also give the man a new perception
   of how his behavior is viewed by others."[9]

4. Get some counseling at a rape crisis center, with a clergy
   person, or from the National Sexual Assault Hotline

(1-800-656-HOPE). "Women who get counseling get over their experiences faster and with fewer lasting effects than those who get no help."[10]

It embarrasses me to learn from rape experts that women who have been raped listed clergy persons as the least helpful.[11] Traditionally, pastors and clerics have told victims that it is their fault, and that the men in their lives have the power to do what they want. However, in my book the days of submission and domination are over. Women must stand up for themselves.

Real men don't rape. It is *never* OK to force yourself on a woman, even if

- She teases you.

- She dresses provocatively or leads you on.

- She says "no" and you think she means "yes."

- You've had sex with her before.

- You've paid for her dinner or given her expensive gifts.

- You think women enjoy being forced to have sex or want to be persuaded.

- The woman is under the influence of alcohol or drugs.[12]

Ladies, there are lessons for you as well.

- Don't send mixed messages—yes means yes and no means no.

- Know your boundaries; if you don't want to be touched, say so at the first touch.

- Decide if you want to have sex or not. I recommend that you abstain, but your intentions should be clear early on.

- If things get out of hand, be loud in protesting, leave, and go for help.

- Avoid falling for such lines as "If you loved me you would."

- Have your own transportation, taxi, or bus fare.

- Avoid secluded places where you are in a vulnerable position.

- Be careful when you invite someone to your home or vice versa.[13]

We ended this proactive Love Clinic, as we did the others, standing on the Word of God. We know that when we do face the pain of life, the power of Jesus goes right with us. In 2 Corinthians 4:7–9 we read, *But we have this treasure in earthen vessels, so that the surpassing greatness of the power will be of God and not from ourselves; we are afflicted in every way, but not crushed, perplexed, but not despairing, persecuted but not forsaken, struck down, but not destroyed.*

Let us pray
Dear God,
Pain and suffering seem to be our permanent address. We need You to be our burden bearer and our heavy load sharer.

We need You to be the lifter of our heads and our way makers. Bind up our wounds and lead us on, in Jesus' name, we pray.
Amen

Chapter 23

RING AROUND THE CLERGY COLLAR RINSES CLEAN WITH CONFESSION

A pastor on the prowl is lethal. He is lethal because he is committing sins under the guise of the Lord and usually gets away with it. Who can say no to God's man, when he requests something, anything? Who would suspect God's messenger of doing anything untoward? These men can use their pastoral license as a passport to peace or to perversion. Their liquid gold voices can soothe or stimulate. Their eyes can beckon one to rescue or to romance. Their gentle touch comforts or arouses. Clergy indiscretions occur because clergy persons are made of flesh. Flesh is not perfect. Yet clergy are traditionally held to a higher standard that does not permit errors. Life on the pedestal is a constant challenge. Clergy bask in the limelight of personal perfection, while they anguish with their own failings and shortcomings.

Clergy sexual misconduct can be defined as "clergy engaging

in sexual or romantic relationships with parishioners or coun-
selees."[1] Doing so is a misuse of power, a violation of the trusting
bond that is the foundation of a healthy pastoral relationship.
Pastoral sexual misconduct can take many forms, sexual contact
and sexual abuse. Victims can be male or female, young or old.

> Statistics indicate that somewhere from one out of eight to one
> out of three clergy have crossed the sexual boundaries with their
> parishioners. Over 76 percent of clergy in another study reported
> knowing of a minister who had sexual intercourse with a pa-
> rishioner.[2]

Some people believe that the church's dirty little secrets
should remain hidden. To reveal the secret disturbs not only the
perpetrator, but also the co-conspirators and the victims. They'd
rather leave well enough alone. When the Love Clinic dared to
speak the words "Ring Around the Clergy Collar" on radio public service announcements and live interviews, we broke the silence and felt the public's wrath. We felt the fire and received
hostile reactions, such as How dare you? Don't throw stones.
Turn your head. Pretend you don't see. Keep on forgiving. He's
only a man, he makes mistakes. Touch not mine anointed.

When clergy misconduct occurs, it creates chaos in three areas: the life of the pastor, the life of the victim, and the life of
the church. Chaos in the pastor's life stems from the fact that
he has forsaken his role of respect and honor. He has thrown
off the mantle of godliness in a lust-driven quest for sex. Some-
where in the back of his mind, he knows that he is wrong, but
he just can't help himself. The tremendous pressures, coupled
with little counseling support, make some types of failure in-

evitable. Some pastors involved in this behavior are crying out for help through their misconduct. Many of them want to be caught so they can finally receive help.

The congregation experiences chaos when the episode is swept under the rug and the victim is silenced or censured. A condition of confidentiality is imposed, collusion is embraced, and business goes on as usual. The silence within the church teaches us that inappropriate behavior is acceptable when it comes from the pastor. It also teaches us that victims have no rights in the church. If the congregation appropriately handles the abuse by disciplining the shepherd, even though it is correct, it is also disheartening and discouraging.

The victims are confused and confounded. They usually experience anger, grief, and shame because they simply cannot believe that their pastor abused them. They trusted, even adored their pastors, and the misconduct shocked them personally and spiritually. The long-lasting affects of clergy misconduct are staggering. Those affects range from depression and the inability to maintain healthy relationships to completely abandoning Christianity.

This Love Clinic was born out of our mission to heal. Just as we clean up the pews, the pulpit warrants a rinse, too. What type of world would we have if our congregations were clean, but our pastors were tainted? Ring around the clergy collar rinses clean with confession, counseling and accountability.

∽ Case 1 ∾

Delores had come with something to say and she was going to say it. This 45-year-old single mother of three had been

wronged in the house of the Lord. Nobody would listen back
then, but things were different now. The words tumbled out of
her mouth excitedly, almost uncontrollably.

"I tried to ignore it. I could not believe it was happening,"
she recounted with pain in her voice. "So I moved farther away
from him. But I was not sitting that close to him in the first
place. He kept scooting over to get next to me. And I knew it
was not right," she raced on.

"Let me slow down and tell the story right," Delores said,
taking a big breath to calm herself down. "The counseling session started off wrong. I called because I needed biblical advice
about my divorce, and how my ex is hassling me. Pastor sched-
uled the appointment personally. His secretary usually does all
of that, plus she or someone is always sitting in the room next
door. Pastor had me to come for counseling when the whole
church was empty. There were just a few deacons having a
meeting down the hall. Everything was real quiet. Instead of
him sitting behind his desk as he usually does, he asked me to
sit with him on the sofa in the corner. Silly me, I sat there. He
is my pastor. He has always been a man of integrity and honor.
He can preach up a storm, too. He even baptized my kids—so
I thought nothing of his change of plans," she explained.

Delores is the fifth of seven girls who were raised in a
working-class home filled with love and church-life, Bible study,
and prayer meetings. Daddy ruled the house with an iron hand.
Men were the heads of women, and the heads of churches. The
girls were taught to give unquestioned loyalty to the pastor specifically, and to men in general. "When Pastor's hand grabbed
my breast for the second time during the counseling session, I'd
had enough. The first time may have been an accident. But the
second time was intentional. And I don't play that! I got up and

ran out of his office screaming, 'Help me!' I ran to the deacons' meeting. I told them what happened but they looked at me like I was speaking a foreign language."

Little did Delores know, she'd entered a twilight zone of sorts where reality is ignored and fantasy reigns. The deacons barely glanced up from their meeting table as she frantically sought their help. Once she left, her words evaporated from their minds like fresh rain on hot pavement. They went on with their meeting as if nothing had happened. In their minds, nothing did. Subsequently, Delores registered another complaint, and was promptly asked to move her membership to another church. The deacons never approached the pastor about the incident. Consequently, his routine of groping and grabbing went undisturbed. Delores was not his first victim. She would not be his last.

"I was truly put out by the whole matter. No one at the church wanted to hear what I had to say. My own church members treated me like some kind of traitor. They questioned my character. Rumors started flying all over about me. They talked about me like a dog. Shoot. I quit going to that church or any church. What kind of mess is that to happen in God's house?"

∽ Diagnosis ∾

I told her, "You were very brave to speak up, Sister Delores. We have heard you. You have spoken well, not only for you but also for the women who can't speak up. Some women do not have the guts to protest. Some of them can't speak up because they are afraid, or because the pastor's attention makes them feel special, or because they are sworn to secrecy. Your self-esteem would not let you just sit there and be a victim."

An incident like this can put a woman into spiritual confusion. Defending oneself against an authority figure who is supposed to help is confusing. This pastor abused his clerical power and authority. He was her spiritual guide and he misused his influence as he foisted his sexual interest in her into the context of a counseling session. Her spirituality was trampled. She trusted God, the church, and her pastor. She was betrayed. But not only was she betrayed by her pastor, she was betrayed by her church community—the deacons who would not listen, and the church members who whispered about her. That pastor stole from her trust, devotion and a portion of her faith in God.

"When a pastor violates a parishioner's boundaries he is stealing from her the appropriate, powerful, and sustaining relationships of spiritual guidance and support that the church has represented to her."[3] Delores was spiritually robbed.

∽ Prescription ∽

The pastor saw Delores as a target. To him, she was an easy sex tool. I suspect that her docile demeanor in the presence of men contributed to the pastor's ability to so easily rob her. Unfortunately, we can't be too trusting with anybody, even at church. Don't let your guard down. Follow your gut instincts. If it feels wrong, don't go any further. Counselors have put together a profile of what a potential victim looks like. Here are some pitfalls to avoid: "She is socialized to be polite, not confrontational, accepting of men's behavior, trained to heal men's wounds, submissiveness to men."[4]

You will be a target no longer. I recommend development in the area of self-assertion and learning to say no. I recommend that you spend time in the scriptures and reflect on the power of God who specializes in helping those who have been wounded by powerful, harmful people. In Psalm 118:5–7 we can read, *From my distress I called upon the Lord; the Lord answered me and set me in a large place. The Lord is for me; I will not fear; What can man do to me? The Lord is for me among those who help me; therefore I shall look with satisfaction on those who hate me.*

God gives us the strength to press on and to make sure that we have the guts to keep on standing up for ourselves.

∽ Case 2 ∾

Tremendous healing for victims can take place when a perpetrator comes forward to admit his guilt. It does not always have to be the original offender. An apology goes a long way to someone who is hurting. It was amazing to hear the other side of the story. After a number of women spoke of their victimization, the Rev. Cleotus came to the microphone to talk. The small, wry man of 60-plus with a head of gray hair and a beard to match seized our attention. His traditional black suit, cross pendent, and large rimmed glasses gave him the look of the historically revered shepherd. All of his life he had desperately sought the veneration and respect automatically given to men of the cloth. Yet he always stood in the shadows of his father, a prominent bishop. He never quite met his father's demanding expectations. Ministry had been a struggle for him. His churches had stumbled and faltered along over the years.

"I've not been all the things I should have been as a pastor," he said. "I've done some things wrong in my life and in my church. My attitude has not been right. I let things get out of hand. And I was wrong," he said. "My problem is that I have not treated the women in my churches correctly. I'm a sinner and I'm tired of pretending that my life is perfect. Guilt is a monster. The Bible says that if we confess our sins to one another we will be forgiven. I need to be forgiven."

Over the decades of his ministry, Rev. Cleotus developed a trail of unhealthy generational sexual relationships with female church members. Some of the women were from the same family. His wife turned a deaf ear and blind eye to it all so that she could hold onto her title as the first lady. Their children grew up in the household of denial, and also pretended that nothing was happening. Occasionally paternity suits or other sexual allegations arose, but they were quickly squelched by the loyal church leaders.

Rev. Cleotus continued slowly, recounting the roots of his pain. "When I first started out in the ministry, the older preachers in my family took me under their wings. They taught me how to run a church, how to pastor people, and how to preach. I was grateful, because they brought me into manhood. There was one lesson that they told me that I took to heart. 'Son,' they said, 'every rat has at least two holes to go in. It's a poor one that only has one.' I am not a poor rat." He beamed. "They were talking about the women of their churches. I was instructed to make the women of my church all mine," he concluded. "I wanted to be the pastor and those were the requirements. Lives have been ruined. I didn't care for a long time. Now I do."

∽ Diagnosis ∾

"The stains on clergy are not meant to be permanent. We all stumble and fall at some point," I told Rev. Cleotus. While we were relieved by his confession, that was only the beginning of his healing. I wondered if he wanted to take it beyond mere talk. I said, "Your penitence is the vehicle for your healing and ultimate change. As I listened to your testimony, I heard some pain concerning your relationship with your father. The disappointments that came from the poor relationships and the struggles in your ministry must have produced large amounts of anxiety inside you, as well as a feeling of loss. I suggest that the sexual sins were an attempt to gain control and accumulate accomplishments in your life. You may be experiencing a wound known as narcissism."

> Narcissism impairs a ministers' professional judgment in a way that puts him particularly at risk for crossing boundaries, because it damages his capacity for empathy and causes him to seek gratification of his own needs first, regardless of the cost to others.[5]

I continued, "This means that you are wounded. Ministers and pastors are known as wounded healers, a term created by theologian Henri Nouwen. It means that all of us have inner, emotional wounds from painful life experiences. Nouwen suggests that pastors are drawn to the work of healing because we understand being wounded from inside the experience.[6] The intensity of a particular wound determines whether or not we will abuse our flocks.[7] Other contributing factors are stress, depression, marital discord, isolation, burnout, and overcommitment."

☙ **Prescription** ☙

Therapy and counseling will be the most effective methods of ending this nightmare. There are pastoral counseling groups in his city. The wounds will not go away by themselves, and it will be very beneficial for him to gain specialized education that emphasizes not just what he did, but how he thinks about himself, his strengths and weaknesses, his role as clergy, and issues of gender, power, and authority.[8] This education would also have him revisit his understanding of women and their rights not to be abused or used for another's personal gratification. Their boundaries should never be crossed, especially by their pastor.

Some good advice for anyone, including pastors, is to take better care of the inner you: Don't let others cross your boundaries, eat properly, get enough sleep, and exercise regularly. Don't overschedule your days—leave time to reflect and relax. Don't allow your work, even if it is God's work, to consume who you are. Pray for yourself. Clergy are often asked to take care of others' needs, but they also need to pay attention to their own.

Cleotus needs to help his congregation begin the healing process. His willingness to face the issue can lead to fixing it.

No minister can save anyone. He can only offer himself as a guide to fearful people. Yet paradoxically, it is precisely in this guidance that the first signs of hope become visible . . . A Christian community is therefore a healing community not because wounds are cured and pains are alleviated, but because wounds and pains become openings or occasions for a new vision.[9]

We closed this session by thanking God for our pastors, preachers, elders, and bishops and the important role that they have in our lives. In Romans 10:14 we read, *How then will they call on Him in whom they have not believed? And how shall they believe in Him whom they have not heard? And how will they hear without a preacher? How will they preach unless they are sent? Just as it is written, "How beautiful are the feet of those who bring good news of good things!"*

Let us pray
Dear God,
Thank You for our shepherds, they are mighty men and women whom You have selected. Give us the power to take care of them. Give them the power to take care of themselves.
Amen

Chapter 24

JESUS IS THE ONLY HIGH YOU NEED

Christians are addicted to drugs, alcohol, sex, shopping, and more, like the rest of the world. Just because there is a cross around our neck and a Bible in our hand doesn't mean we can't get hooked on something and not be able to let go. Simply put, addictions are the habitual use of a substance or behavior. The desire for "it" becomes more important than anything or anybody in the world. When you add an addiction to a Christian love relationship, you have some hell in the household, because the addict's loyalty is always going to be to the high. Addicts must decide daily where their next high is going to come from. Those who love them must decide how long to hold on to the addict, or whether they should.

When one loves a drug addict, the relationship is weighed down with destructive behavior. First there is the deception. An addict will spin a web of lies to cover up the disappearance of money, the days unaccounted for, and the inappropriate behavior. An addict will deny, blame, minimize, and rationalize and be unable or unwilling to confess that he or she is hooked. Anger spews forth if they are confronted, followed by increasing anger if they are not believed.

Addicts exist in the church due to the church's fear of intervention. It's easier to whisper about them behind their backs or in a gossiping phone call after service. Addicts become further entrenched into their habits because we don't confront them, demand they get help, and point to Jesus as the solution. The Scriptures tell us, in Galatians 6:1, *Brethren, even if anyone is caught in any trespass, you who are spiritual, restore such a one in a spirit of gentleness; each one looking to yourself, so you too will not be tempted.*

Not only doesn't the church extend a helping hand, but the family of an addict must endure the gauntlet of painful questions about their addicted loved one. Which rehab is she in this time? If I were you, I'd have him arrested. What kind of parent are you to put up with that? I would not have that in my house. He didn't take your jewelry again?

The Love Clinic that focused on addiction was awesome because, as this relatively invisible illness took form before our eyes, it reinforced the truth that Jesus is the only high that you need.

∞ **Case 1** ∞

Maria, 28, loves a crackhead. He is her husband. This drug ravaged their ten-year marriage. His crack habit has created a relentless wedge between them. He uses. They split up. He promises to leave crack alone. Then they get back together. He starts to use again. They break up. He promises once more. They reunite. They came to the Love Clinic to talk about their situation and offer help to others. No, they were not healed, but the communion of the community made them feel better.

"My jewelry has all been pawned, including the wedding rings that I worked a second job to buy," said Maria, an administrative assistant. "Electrical appliances and stereo equipment in our apartment have long since made their exit. But our love is here. And love is all I need, as long as I have him. I don't care what anyone says about him. He is mine."

Demarcus, Maria's 29-year-old husband, stepped forward. "I love my wife dearly. I'm worried that I love the coke pipe more," he said. "I want them both, and sometimes I want one more than the other. Most of the time I wish that God would strengthen me to do the right thing. Maria is great to have stayed with me through all of this. I know that I can put down the drugs if she stays with me."

"Everyone has a cross to bear," continued Maria. "This is mine. I do believe that he will get clean one day. He told me he has the strength to put the pipe down. I know he can. If I walk away now, it will be just like giving up on God. I can't leave God."

∽ Diagnosis ∾

Life hands us unexpected hardships, but if we can manage to stick together that is half of the battle. This couple was in way over their heads, but I had a good feeling about them. Their marriage has the potential to be the bright spot in the midst of the addiction. The fact that they've been able to hold on to each other is significant. It demonstrates their commitment to each other and to the marriage. Marriage can be a safety net or co-coon for you both that can withstand the difficulties down the road. However, they needed to be aware of the dangers of co-dependence. His addiction could be her downfall.

∞ Prescription ∞

I shared with Maria, "Sister, you must first get help for yourself in a group like Al-Anon, and other co-dependency groups. Loving an addict is probably the most difficult type of love there is, because you run the risk of becoming co-dependent. You and Demarcus are in a kind of sick, whirling dance. You are holding tight to a lover who does you no good, and causes you pain. Your sickness is that the pain feels good, and when there is no pain you feel bad," I said. "Your situation will probably get worse before it gets better. His healing may begin when you get help."

I told Demarcus, "True love would not be hindered by drugs. If you love your wife, you will love yourself enough to get into treatment. Right now, your love is divided between her and the drug. And as a result you are being torn apart. As an addict, you are more than likely living in a world of denial. Most addicts say they can quit anytime, but they are fooling themselves. You can fool us, but not God. Please, get some help," I said.

"As a couple, also seek counseling. Lasting recovery will require that the marriage not be one of co-dependence. The drug addiction has warped your love for each other. You are doing negative things you never thought that you'd do. Together you can reverse the direction that you are headed in."

∞ **Case 2** ∞

Addicts come in all shapes and sizes. When mild-mannered church librarian Madeline came forward to testify, we were shocked. She is a part of a burgeoning population of addicts who'd never be suspected of looking for a high. They are the abusers of legal drugs. These addicts started with their drug of choice when it was prescribed by their doctors. "The principle of addiction is simple; pain + relief = dependency."[1]

At 51, Madeline is part of the group most at risk for legal drug abuse—middle-aged women.[2] She had been feeling lonely and anxious when her children left for college. The empty-nest syndrome set in and Madeline lost her personal focus and energy for life. She went to her physician complaining of anxiety and was given a prescription for Valium. "I enjoy the feeling that they give me. I am free of worry about my children, or about my life. I just don't worry anymore," she explained. "The problem is that my doctor wants me to stop taking them. He says that they have outlived their usefulness, but I see it differently."

Madeline was using the drugs as an escape from her reality. Unfortunately, she was escaping more and more frequently, and when she returned she was more miserable than before. She missed days of work, and she was undependable when she did show up. She was not the same person.

∞ **Diagnosis** ∞

"Madeline," I said, "you are convinced that you cannot make it without the pills, but you can. They have become a part of your daily routine. Taking one to get going, and another to keep going is a concerning habit. I don't want you to be too hard on yourself. There are hosts of factors in our lives that drag us down to this point. If you are too self-critical, you may not be able to build the momentum needed to help. You'll wind up hosting your own pity party."

> [Many women] feel torn between the inner world of their own perceptions of reality and the outer world, socially constructed and interpreted by men . . . Often it is difficult for a woman to distinguish her own truth from a culturally fabricated version of who she is and who she ought to be.[3]

"Your confusion may have led to an anger and a need to manifest that in self-destructive behavior," I said.

∞ Prescription ∞

Pray and seek God's protection and support for the strength to quit. To come out of any addiction you will have to undergo a period of detoxification under the supervision of a physician or at a hospital. This process can take weeks depending on the drug and will probably be painful. Therapy is my second rec-ommendation because withdrawal from the drug involves emo-tional disturbances such as depression, anxiety, and mood swings.[4] You will need support and counseling to deal with the disturbances.

We ended this Love Clinic celebrating the possibilities of free-dom in the name of Jesus. In John 8:32, the Bible tells us, *and you will know the truth and the truth will make you free.*

Let us pray

Dear God,

We lift up addicts and families of addicts. Let them know that there is still hope. Keep them from languishing in the pit of despair. Shine the light of possibilities into their hearts. Amen

PROGNOSIS

I believe the angel who told Mary, the mother of Jesus, *For nothing will be impossible with God* (Luke 1:37). Nothing is impossible in our relationships because of the power of God. That's why I am full of hope for you and your situation. You must believe that God is with you and you will make it through the difficulties and to the place of peace God has designed for you. The Love Clinic is based on the unshakeable conviction that God cares for God's people. Our love relationships are a priority for God, because God is love.

This visit to the Love Clinic has affected you for the better. You now understand that you are not alone—others have gone through your particular storm and emerged victorious, just as you will. You've been given counsel and advice based on the Word of God. Therefore, a full recovery is expected. The future looks positive for your relationships, if you follow the doctor's orders.

1. Study what the Bible teaches about love.

2. Pray that God will empower you to love as you should.

3. Strive to live the love that God wants for you.

4. Take a realistic look at all of your relationships to determine if they are healthy and positive. If they are not, take action to change them or yourself.

5. Remember that love is always the answer.

Please come back for your next check-up soon.

ENDNOTES

CHAPTER 1

1. Larry Davis. "Factors Contributing to Partner Commitment among Unmarried African Americans," *Social Work Research* 24 (2000): 4–12.
2. Ibid.
3. Suzan D. Johnson Cook. *A New Dating Attitude* (Grand Rapids, MI: Zondervan, 2001), 59.
4. Erma Jean Lawson and Aaron Thompson. *Black Men and Divorce* (London: Sage, 1999), 19.
5. Don Raunnikar. *Choosing God's Best* (Sisters, OR: Multnomah Books, 1998), 146.
6. Ibid, 162.
7. Sheron C. Patterson, *Ministry with Black Single Adults* (Nashville, TN: Discipleship Resources, 1995), 41.

CHAPTER 2

1. Carol Saussy, *God Images and Self Esteem: Empowering Women in a Patriarchal Society* (Louisville, Ky: Westminster/John Knox Press, 1991), 16, 147.
2. Ibid., 147.

CHAPTER 3

1. Lawrence E. Gary, *Black Men* (Newbury Park, Calif.: Sage), 88.
2. Ibid.
3. William July II, *Brothers, Lust and Love* (Houston: Khufu Books), 65.
4. Ibid.
5. Catherine Clark Kroger and James R. Beck, *Healing the Hurting: Giving Hope and Help to Abused Women* (Grand Rapids, Mich.: Baker House), 84.
6. Ibid., 85.
7. Ibid., 91.
8. Ibid.
9. Ibid.
10. Ibid.

CHAPTER 4

1. George Edmond Smith, *More Than Sex* (New York: Kensington Books, 2000), 171.

CHAPTER 5

1. Gwendolyn Goldsby Grant, *The Best Kind of Loving* (New York: Harper Perennial, 1995), 217.
2. Ibid., 218.

CHAPTER 6

1. Donald D. Hensrud, "How to Live Longer," *Fortune* 143 (2001), 210.
2. Steve Brody and Cathey Brody, *Renew Your Marriage Midlife* (New York: Putnam, 1999), 32.
3. Ibid., 32–33.
4. Authur H. Becker, *Ministry with Older Persons* (Minneapolis: Augsburg, 1986), 24.
5. Ibid., 48.
6. Ibid., 171.
7. Greg, Gutfeld, "Why We Love Older Women," *Men's Health* 15 (2000), 120.
8. T. D. Jakes, *Woman, Thou Art Loosed* (Tulsa, Okla.: Albury, 1996), 187.
9. Ibid.

CHAPTER 7

1. Stephanie Staal, "Warning, Living Together May Ruin Your Relationship," *Cosmopolitan* 231 (2001), 286.
2. Ibid.
3. Ibid.
4. Ibid.
5. Don Rannikar, *Choosing God's Best* (Sisters, Oreg.: Multnomah Books, 1998), 58.
6. Ibid., 71.
7. Ibid., 96.
8. T. R. Eng and W. T. Butler, *The Hidden Epidemic: Confronting Sexually Transmitted Diseases* (Washington, D.C.: National Academy Press, 1997), 216.
9. Clarence Walker, *Breaking Strongholds in the African American Family* (Grand Rapids, Mich.: Zondervan, 1996), 13.
10. Ibid., 16.
11. Jakes, *Woman, Thou Art Loosed*, 112.

CHAPTER 8

1. Pat Love, *The Truth about Love* (New York: Fireside Books, 2001), 29.
2. Joan and Richard Hunt, *Growing Love in Christian Marriage* (Nashville, Tenn.: Abingdon Press, 1981), 61.
3. bell hooks, *Salvation, Black People and Love* (New York: William Morrow, 2001), 125.
4. John M. Gottman, *The Seven Principles for Making Marriage Work* (New York: Crown, 1999), 190.
5. Ibid., 191.
6. Dick Dunn, *Willing to Try Again* (Valley Forge, Pa.: Judson Press, 1993), back cover.
7. Ibid., 5.
8. Ibid., 8.
9. Ibid., 9.
10. Ibid., 104.

CHAPTER 9

1. Melba Colgrove, Harold H. Bloomfield, and Peter McWilliams, *How to Survive the Loss of a Love: 58 Things to Do Where There Is Nothing to Be Done* (Los Angeles: Prelude Press, 1976), 19.

2. Dwight Webb, *50 Ways to Love Your Leaver* (Atascadero, Calif.: Impact, 2000), 9.
3. Ibid., 16.
4. Ibid., 15.
5. Colgrove et al., *How to Survive*, 46.
6. Ibid., 150.
7. Howard W. Stone, *Depression and Hope* (Minneapolis: Fortress Press, 1998), 146.
8. Ibid.
9. Ibid., 44.

CHAPTER 10
1. Smith, *More Than Sex*, 154.
2. Ibid.
3. Gottman, *Seven Principles*, 27.
4. Ibid.
5. Ibid., 28.
6. Ibid., 29.
7. Ibid., 33.
8. Ibid., 89.
9. Gary Chapman, *The Five Love Languages* (Chicago: Northfield, 1995), 19.
10. Ibid., 14.
11. Ibid., 38.
12. Ibid., 104.

CHAPTER 11
1. Dave Carder, "Why Affairs Happen," *Marriage Prevention* 18 (2001), 30.
2. Ibid.
3. Ibid., 31.
4. Pamela Cooper-White, *The Cry of Tamar: Violence against Women on the Church's Response* (Minneapolis: Fortress Press, 1995), 157.
5. Cardner, "Affairs," 31.
6. Ibid.
7. Ibid., 32.
8. Pamela Johnson, "Are You Cheating?" *Essence* 31 (January 2001), 102.

9. Carner, "Affairs," 32.
10. J. Allan Petersen, *The Myth of the Greener Grass* (Wheaton, Ill.: Tyndale House, 1991), 77.
11. Smith, *More Than Sex*, 53.

CHAPTER 12

1. Michele Weiner Davis, *The Divorce Remedy* (New York: Simon & Schuster, 2001), 193.
2. Petersen, *Myth of the Greener Grass*, 115.
3. Ibid., 110.
4. Davis, *Divorce Remedy*, 195.
5. Petersen, *Myth*, 196.
6. Davis, *Divorce Remedy*, 206.
7. Ibid., 217.

CHAPTER 13

1. Jim Smoke, *Growing through Divorce* (Eugene, Oreg.: Harvest House, 1995), 40.
2. Ibid., 26.

CHAPTER 14

1. Linda J. Waite and Maggie Gallagher, *The Case for Marriage* (New York: Doubleday, 2001), 78.
2. Ibid., 96.
3. Ibid.
4. Ibid., 89.
5. Ibid., 79.
6. Ibid.
7. Joan Avna and Diana Waltz, *Celibate Wives* (Los Angeles: Lowell House, 1992), 5.
8. Ibid., 104.
9. Ibid., 104, 198.
10. William F. Harley Jr., *His Needs Her Needs* (Grand Rapids, Mich.: Fleming Revell, 1997), 44.
11. Avna and Waltz, *Celibate Wives*, 105.
12. Harley, *His Needs*, p. 32.
13. Smith, *More Than Sex*, 125.

14. Ibid., 123, 126.
15. Ibid., 125.

CHAPTER 15
1. *The United Methodist Hymnal* (Nashville, Tenn.: The United Methodist Publishing House, 1993), 867.
2. Waite and Gallagher, *Case for Marriage*, 68.
3. Davis, *Divorce Remedy*, 54.
4. Millner and Chiles, *Money, Power, Respect*, 6–7.
5. Waite and Gallagher, *Case for Marriage*, 99.
6. Sheron C. Patterson, *New Faith: The Black Woman's Guide to Reformation, Re-Creation, Rediscovery, Renaissance, Resurrection and Revival* (Minneapolis: Fortress Press, 2000), 124.
7. Ibid., 129.

CHAPTER 16
1. Barbara Dycus, *God's Design for Broken Lives* (Springfield, Mo.: Chrism Books, 1994), 146.
2. *Jet* "Is Divorce Hurting the Children?" *Jet* 92, (1998) 15.
3. Dycus, *God's Design*, 132.
4. Ibid., 132.
5. Smoke, *Growing through Divorce*, 64.

CHAPTER 17
1. Ralph Earle, Gregory Crow, and Kevin Osborn, *Lonely All the Time: Recognizing, Understanding, and Overcoming Sex Addictions for Addicts and Co-Dependents* (New York: Pocket Books, 1989), 5.
2. Betsy Morris, "Addicted to Sex," *Fortune*, May 1999, 69.
3. Earle et al., *Lonely*, 3.
4. Ibid., 16.
5. Ibid., 4.
6. Ibid., 100.
7. Ibid., 108.
8. Ibid.
9. Ibid., 86.
10. Ibid., 18.
11. Ibid., 87.
12. Ibid., 222.

CHAPTER 18

1. "Teen Moms and Dads," *Christian Science Monitor*, 8 June 2001 p. 10.
2. Gail Elizabeth Wyatt, *Stolen Women* (New York: John Wiley & Sons, 1997), 93.
3. "Teen Moms and Dads."
4. Wyatt, *Stolen Women*, 97.
5. Ibid., 102.
6. "Teen Moms and Dads."
7. G. Wade Rowatt Jr., *Adolescents in Crisis* (Louisville, Ky.: Westminster/John Knox Press, 2001), 98.
8. Grant, *Best Kind of Loving* 148.
9. Ibid., 150.

CHAPTER 19

1. Eric Brandt, editor, *Dangerous Liaisons: Blacks, Gays, and the Struggle for Equality* (New York: The New Press, 1999), 292.
2. David K. Switzer, *Pastoral Care of Gays, Lesbians, and Their Families* (Minneapolis: Fortress Press, 1999), 87.
3. Ibid., 139.
4. Ibid., 140.
5. Ibid., 115.
6. Brandt, *Dangerous Liaisons*, 163.
7. Switzer, *Pastoral Care*, 121.

CHAPTER 20

1. Michael J. Christensen, *The Samaritan's Imperative* (Nashville: Abingdon Press, 1991), 139.
2. Ibid., 139.
3. Ibid., 151.
4. Ibid., 197.

CHAPTER 21

1. The Commonwealth Fund, First Comprehensive National Health Survey of American Women, July 1993.
2. The Commonwealth Fund, Health Concerns Across A Woman's Life Span: The Commonwealth Fund 1998 Survey of Women's Health, May 1998.

3. Conversation with counselor at the Genesis Women's Shelter, Dallas Texas 2002.
4. Catherine Clark Kroger and James R. Beck, *Healing the Hurting* (Grand Rapids, Mich. Baker Books), 167.

CHAPTER 22

1. Emilie M. Townes, editor, *A Troubling in My Soul* (Maryknoll, N.Y.: Orbis Books, 1993), 109.
2. Linda H. Hollies, *Mother Goose Meets a Woman Called Wisdom* (Cleveland, Ohio: United Church Press, 2000), 96.
3. Edward K. Rowell, editor, *Quotes and Idea Starters for Preaching and Teaching* (Grand Rapids, Mich.: Baker Books, 1996), 161.
4. Jean O'Gorman Hughes and Bernice R. Sandler, *"Friends" Raping Friends—Could It Happen to You?* (Washington, D.C.: Project on the Status and Education of Women, Association of American Colleges, 1987). Available online at www.eon.anglia.ac.uk./DOVI/articles/article 13.htm.
5. Ibid.
6. Ibid.
7. Ibid.
8. Ibid.
9. Ibid.
10. Ibid.
11. Ibid.
12. Ibid.
13. Ibid.

CHAPTER 23

1. Cooper-White, *Cry of Tamar*, 128.
2. Ibid., 128.
3. Ibid., 131.
4. Ibid., 134.
5. Ibid., 137.
6. Ibid., 195.
7. Ibid., 137.
8. Ibid.
9. Ibid., 201.

CHAPTER 24

1. Bridget Clare McKeever, *Hidden Addictions* (New York: The Haworth Pastoral Press, 1998), 23.
2. Ibid., 7.
3. Ibid., 55.
4. Ibid., 67.

INDEX

Page numbers in **bold** indicate charts.

Abusive relationships, 183–89
    conflicting feelings about, 187–89
    leaving abusive relationships, 186–87
    love, symbolized as abuse, 187–89
    survivors of, 189
    women batterers, 184–87
Acceptance
    of AIDS, 180
    of divorce, 117–19
Acknowledging problem, 152–53, 156
Acquaintance rape, 191–97
Actions
    changing unhealthy relationships, 219
    consequences of, 61
    listening to, 33–35
Addiction, 211–17
    church and addicts, 21
    counseling for, 214, 216
    drug addicts, loving, 212–14
    legal drug addicts, 215–16
    middle-aged women and, 215–16
    recovery, 214
    See also Freaks
Adultery, 94–103
    attractions of, 95
    Class One affairs, 95
    Class Three affairs, 95

Class Two affairs, 95
    emotion affairs, 96–99
    generational cause of problem, 95
    serial adulterer, 99–102
    temptation and, 99–102
    See also Caught spouse in the act
Affairs (extramarital), 95. *See also*
        Adultery; Caught spouse in the act
African Americans
    homosexuals and, 168, 172
    teen pregnancy, 161
AIDS, 176–82
    acceptance, 180
    blood transfusion, 180–82
    church and, 177–78, 180
    denial, 180
    depression, 180
    emotions, range of, 179–80
    God and, 180, 181
    homophobia and, 168–69, 176
    redemption from chronic illness, 181–
        82
    spousal betrayal and, 178–80
American Sociological Association, 140
Anger
    divorce, anger from, 115–17

Anger *(cont.)*
  forgiveness and, 17–21
Attractions of adultery, 95

Baby-makers, 165–66
Balance for single parents, 144–46
Beginning conversations, importance of, 86
Bible teachings on love, 219
Blended families, 71–73
Blood transfusion and AIDS, 180–82
Body language and communication, 89
Boundaries with families, creating, 70
Breaking Stronghold in the African American Family (Walker), 61
Breakups, 75–83
  depression, 81–82
  family breakups, 79–82
  forgiveness and, 79
  grieving and men, 76–79
  joint counseling, 82
  rejection, 78
  See also Ending relationships
Brokenness and teen pregnancy, 162
Burns, Kephra, 134

CARE decision-making, 163
Caring for love, 131–32
Caught spouse in the act, 104–12
  cyber addict, 106–9
  fighting reaction, 105
  folding reaction, 105
  forgiveness and, 108–9
  freezing reaction, 105
  frying reaction, 105
  immature men, 109–11
  reactions to, 105
  sexually transmitted disease (STD), 60, 109
  surviving infidelity, 104–5
  See also Adultery
Celibacy, 10
Celibate marriage, 122–25
Cheating. *See* Adultery; Caught spouse in the act
Children
  divorce aftermath and, 140–42
  engagements and, 71–73
  senior love and, 48–50
Child state, getting trapped in, 117
Christian dating, 9–10
Church viewpoint
  addicts, 21
  AIDS, 177–78, 180
  homosexuals, 169–71, 172
  meeting others in, 3
Class One affairs, 95
Class Three affairs, 95
Class Two affairs, 95
Clergy misconduct, 200–10

congregation, chaos in, 202
  healing from apology, 206, 209
  narcissism, 206–9
  pastor's life, chaos in, 201–2
  power, misuse of, 200–1
  silence about, 201, 202, 204
  spiritual robbing by, 202–6
  therapy for, 209
  victims of, 202
  wounded healers, 206–9
Cohabitation factor, 54–58. *See also* Shacking
Collaboration vs. headship struggle, 135–38
Commitment of senior love, 47
Communication, 84–93
  beginning conversations, importance of, 86
  body language and, 89
  complaining vs. criticism, 88
  generational cause of problems, 85, 89
  harsh startup, 86–90
  love language, 91–92
  negative interaction, 88
  nonverbal communication, 90–92
  psychological self-hate, 85
  Stress-Reducing Conversation exercise, 89–90
  women vs. men, 84–85, 86
Complaining vs. criticism, 88
Conflicting feelings about abuse, 187–89
Congregation and clergy misconduct, 202
Consumerism of hoochies, 13
Copeland, Shawn, 190
Counseling
  for addicts, 214, 216
  for rape, 196–97
Counterfeit oneness, 54–59
Crying, 191
Cyber addict, 106–9

Dangerous relationships, 36–38
Date rape, 191–97
Dating. *See* Singles
Davis, Michele Weiner, 111
Denial
  of AIDS, 180
  of rape, 194
Depression
  from AIDS, 180
  from breakups, 81–82
Desperation level of singles, 2
Divorce, 113–20
  acceptance of, 117–19
  anger and, 115–17
  child state, getting trapped in, 117
  engagements and, 71–73
  God and, 113–14
  healing from, 116–17

history of divorce, repeating, 140
newness, seeking, 119
past, letting go of, 117
shacking and divorce rates, 54
thermostat vs. thermometer, 117
See also Single parents
Divorced Children's Bill of Rights, 143–44
Divorce Remedy, The (Davis), 111
Dogs, 22–31
emotional distancing, 24–28
misogyny, 28–31
punks, 24
reporting system on, lack of, 23
sexism, 23–24
Domestic violence. *See* Abusive
relationships
Drug addicts, loving, 212–14

Emotion affairs, 96–99
Emotional baggage of singles, 1
Emotional commitment of marital sex, 122
Emotional distancing of men, 24–28
Ending relationships, 32–38
actions, listening to, 33–35
dangerous relationships, 36–38
Personal Bill of Rights, 35–36
See also Breakups
Engagements, 64–74
blended families, 71–73
boundaries with families, creating, 70
children and, 71–73
divorce and, 71–73
intoxication of love, 64–65, 66
parental relationships and, 67–70
premarital counseling and, 64, 65–67
sexual beings, parents as, 72
stepfamilies, 71–73
Essence magazine, 134, 165
Exhibitionists, 149–53
Extramarital affairs. *See* Adultery; Caught
spouse in the act

Fairy tales and faith, 5
Faith and singles, 2, 10
Families
breakups of, 79–82
homosexuals and, 171–74
Fighting reaction to adultery, 105
Flexibility of senior love, 47
Folding reaction to adultery, 105
Forgiveness
adultery, 108–9
breakups, 79
suffering and, 196
Freaks, 147–57
acknowledging problem, 152–53, 156
exhibitionists, 149–53

lust, power of, 151–52, 156
one-night stands, 153–56
porn addiction, 153–56
positive vs. negative sides, 147–48
sex addicts (male and female), 149–56
sexual addictions, 148–49
ultrastrict religious upbringing and, 154
violent upbringing and, 150–51
See also Addiction
Freezing reaction to adultery, 105
Friendship
love from, 9–10
senior love and, 47
Frying reaction to adultery, 105

Gay men. *See* Homosexual Christians
Generational cause
of adultery, 95
of communication problems, 85, 89
of shacking, 60–63
Goal setting importance for teen parents, 162–63
God
AIDS and, 180, 181
divorce and, 113–14
first in relationship, 10
love and, 218–19
sex and, 121–22
voice vs. Satan's voice, 9
See also Love Clinic
Goldsby, Gwen Grant, 165
Graham, Stedman, 134
Grieving and men, 76–79
Ground rules of Love Clinic, xv
Growth of people, friction from, 135–38

Handling suffering, 190
Happiness of married people, 131
Harsh startup of communication, 86–90
Headship struggle vs. collaboration, 135–38
Healing
clergy misconduct, apology for, 206, 209
divorce, 116–17
High-profile women and remaining in
love, 132–35
Hollies, Linda, 191
Homophobia, 168–69, 176
Homosexual Christians, 167–75
African American community and, 168, 172
churches' rejection of, 169–71, 172
families of, 171–74
homophobia, 168–69, 176
Jesus vs. church, 170, 171
suicide, 170–71
hooks, bell, 69

Hoochies, 12–21
  anger and forgiveness, 17–21
  consumerism, 13
  personal power, 16–17
  releasing old self, 15
  second-class role of women, 20–21
  self-preservation, 13

Immature men, 109–11
Impotence, 125–28
Incest, 97–98
Independence, lack of, 2
Infidelity. *See* Adultery; Caught spouse in
  the act
Inhibited sexual desire (ISD), 123–25
Intimacy by sharing feelings, 47
Intoxication of love, 64–65, 66
ISD (inhibited sexual desire), 123–25

Jesus vs. church on homosexuals, 170,
  171
Johnson-Cook, Suzan, 5–6
Joint counseling for breakups, 82
Journal of Psychology and Aging, The,
  46
July, William, 27

Kübler-Ross, Elisabeth, 78

Leaving abusive relationships, 186–87
Legal drug addicts, 215–16
Lesbian women. *See* Homosexual
  Christians
Lessons, learning, 2
Letter writing to attacker, 196
Living together. *See* Shacking
Looking for love, 42
Love
  language, 91–92
  living thing, love as, 131
  symbolized as abuse, 187–89
Love Clinic, xiii–xvi, 218–19
  action to change unhealthy
    relationships, 219
  Bible teachings on love, 219
  God and, 218–19
  ground rules, xv
  prayer, life-altering power of, xvi, 219
  Word of Hope, xv–xvi
  See also Abusive relationships;
    Addiction; Adultery; AIDS; Breakups;
    Caught spouse in the act; Clergy
    misconduct; Communication; Divorce;
    Dogs; Ending relationships;
    Engagements; Freaks; Homosexual
    Christians; Hoochies; Remaining in
    love; Senior love; Sex; Shacking;
    Single parents; Singles; Suffering; Teen
    pregnancy; Waiting for love
Lust, power of, 151–52, 156

Mara mentality, 50–52
Marital sex, 122
Married people, dating, 2
Men
  grieving, 76–79
  immature men, 109–11
  rape and, 197
  sex addicts, 149–56
  sexism of, 23–24
  teen pregnancy and, 163–66
  waiting for love, 43–45
  women vs. communications, 84–85, 86
  See also Dogs
Mentors for teens, 166
Middle-aged women and addiction, 215–
  16
Miscommunication and date rape, 193
Mismatches, intentional, 2
Misogyny, 28–31
Missionary dating, 6–9
Money, friction from, 132–35
Moral standards of singles, 10
More Than Just Sex (Smith), 85
Mortality of married people, 130–31
*Mother Goose Meets a Woman Called
  Wisdom* (Hollies), 191
Mother/smother type, 3–6

Narcissism, 206–9
NASB (New American Standard Bible),
  xvi
National Council on Sexual Addictions
  and Compulsivity, 148
National Sex Survey, 122
National Sexual Assault Hotline, 196–97
Negative interaction, 88
Negative vs. positive sides of people, 147–
  48
New American Standard Bible (NASB),
  xvi
Newlywed seniors, 48–50
Newness, seeking, 119
Nonverbal communication, 90–92

One-night stands, 153–56
Overlooked brother, 42–43

Parental relationships and engagements,
  67–70
Passion and senior love, 47
Past, letting go of, 117
Pastor's life, chaos from misconduct, 201–
  2
Patience and faith, 40–42
Perfectionists, 2

Perkins School of Theology (Southern Methodist University), xiv
Personal Bill of Rights, 35–36
Personal boundaries of singles, 2
Personal power of hoochies, 16–17
Porn addiction, 153–56
Positive vs. negative sides of people, 147–48
Poverty and teen pregnancy, 161
Power of clergy, misuse of, 200–201
Prayer, life-altering power of, xvi, 219
Pregnancy. *See* Teen pregnancy
Premarital counseling, 64, 65–67
Psychological self-hate, 85
Punks, 24

Rape, 191–98
Recovery from addiction, 214
Redemption from chronic illness, 181–82
Rejection from breakups, 78
Releasing old self, 15
Remaining in love, 130–38
  caring for love, 131–32
  growth of people, friction from, 135–38
  happiness of married people, 131
  headship struggle vs. collaboration, 135–38
  high-profile women and, 132–35
  love as living thing, 131
  money, friction from, 132–35
  mortality of married people, 130–31
Reporting system on dogs, lack of, 23
Resolution stage of rape, 194–95
Responsibility for teen pregnancy, 159
Rushing love, 43–45

Satan's voice vs. God's voice, 9
Saussy, Carrol, 20–21
Second-class role of women, 20–21
Self-esteem and sex, 125–28
Self-preservation of hoochies, 13
Senior love, 46–52
  children discouraging, 48–50
  commitment, 47
  flexibility, 47
  friendship and, 47
  intimacy by sharing feelings, 47
  Mara mentality, 50–52
  newlywed seniors, 48–50
  passion and, 47
Serial adulterer, 99–102
Sex, 121–29
  celibate marriage, 122–25
  emotional commitment of marital sex, 122
  God and, 121–22
  impotence, 125–28
  inhibited sexual desire (ISD), 123–25

marital sex, 122
  self-esteem and, 125–28
  sexual dysfunction, 125–28
  singles and, 2
  stress impact on, 123–25
Sex addicts (male and female), 149–56
Sexism of men, 23–24
Sexual beings, parents as, 72
Sexual dysfunction, 125–28
Sexually transmitted disease (STD), 60, 109
Sexual mores (changing) and date rape, 194
Sexual selves, knowledge of, 160, 162
Shacking, 53–63
  actions, consequences of, 61
  cohabitation factor, 54–58
  counterfeit oneness, 54–59
  divorce rates and, 54
  generational stronghold, 60–63
  soul ties, 57
  strongholds, 61–62
Silence about clergy misconduct, 201, 202, 204
Single parents, 139–46
  balance for, 144–46
  children and aftermath of divorce, 140–42
  Divorced Children's Bill of Rights, 143–44
  divorcing history, repeating, 140
  super parents, 145
  See also Divorce
Singles, 1–11
  celibacy, 10
  Christian dating, 9–10
  church for meeting others, 3
  desperation level, 2
  emotional baggage, 1
  fairy tales and faith, 5
  faith and, 2, 10
  friends for love, 9–10
  God as first in relationship, 10
  God's voice vs. Satan's voice, 9
  independence, lack of, 2
  lessons, learning, 2
  married people, dating, 2
  mismatches, intentional, 2
  missionary dating, 6–9
  moral standards, 10
  mother/smother type, 3–6
  perfectionists, 2
  personal boundaries, 2
  sex and, 2
Smith, George Edmond, 85
Socialization and date rape, 193
Soul ties, 57
Southern Methodist University, xiv

Spiritual robbing by clergy misconduct, 202–6
Spousal betrayal and AIDS, 178–80
STD (sexually transmitted disease), 60, 109
Stepfamilies, 71–73
Stress impact on sex, 123–25
Stress-Reducing Conversation exercise, 89–90
Strongholds, 61–62
Suffering, 190–99
    acquaintance rape, 191–97
    counseling for, 196–97
    crying, 191
    date rape, 191–97
    denial stage, 194
    forgiving attacker, 196
    forgiving yourself, 196
    handling suffering, 190
    letter writing to attacker, 196
    men and rape, 197
    miscommunication and date rape, 193
    rape, 191–98
    resolution stage, 194–95
    sexual mores (changing) and date rape, 194
    socialization and date rape, 193
    trauma stage, 194
    victims, 194–95
    women and rape, 197–98
Suicide of homosexuals, 170–71
Super parents, 145
Support groups for teen pregnancy, 163
Surviving
    abuse, 189
    infidelity, 104–5

Taylor, Susan, 134
Teen pregnancy, 158–66
    African Americans vs. Whites, 161
    baby-makers, 165–66
    brokenness and, 162
    CARE decision-making, 163
    goal setting importance, 162–63
    men and, 163–66

    mentors, 166
    poverty and, 161
    responsibility for, 159
    sexual selves, knowledge of, 160, 162
    support groups for, 163
Temptation and adultery, 99–102
Therapy for clergy misconduct, 209
Thermostat vs. thermometer, 117
Trauma stage of rape, 194

Ultrastrict religious upbringing and sexual addictions, 154
University of Wisconsin, 58

Victims
    of clergy misconduct, 202
    of rape, 194–95
Violence. *See* Abusive relationships; Suffering
Violent upbringing and sexual addictions, 150–51

Waiting for love, 39–45
    looking for love, 42
    men waiting for love, 43–45
    overlooked brother, 42–43
    patience and faith, 40–42
    rushing love, 43–45
    women waiting for love, 40–43
Walker, Clarence, 61–62
West, Cornel, 168
Whites and teen pregnancy, 161
Winfrey, Oprah, 134
Women
    batterers, women as, 184–87
    men vs. communication, 84–85, 86
    middle-aged women and addiction, 215–16
    rape and, 197–98
    second-class role of, 20–21
    sex addicts, 149–56
    waiting for love, 40–43
    See also Hoochies
Word of Hope, xv–xvi
Wounded healers, 206–9
Wyatt, Gail, 163

About the Author

Dr. Sheron C. Patterson is the senior pastor of St. Paul United Methodist Church in Dallas, Texas. She is a nationally syndicated radio relationship expert, and the author of five books.

Dr. Patterson is the founder and director of The Love Clinic, a Christian-based institute designed to heal the relationship wounds of our society. Since its inception in 1995, The Love Clinic has produced intriguing seminars and workshops that touch the heart of the matter for adults, teens, college students, and children. For more information about The Love Clinic, please visit www.theloveclinic.com.